POWER
Prayers

for the GRADUATE

D0367496

SHANNA D. GREGOR

BARBOUR
PUBLISHING

Our mission is to publish and distribute inspirational products offering exceptional value and biblical encouragement to the masses.

Member of the
Evangelical Christian
Publishers Association

Dedication

To my wonderful husband,
Blaine, and my two sons, Brady and Bryce.
It is such a joy to pray for each of you.

Contents

Introduction

The Power of Prayer

*"You had no sooner started your prayer when the answer
was given. And now I'm here to deliver the answer to you.
You are much loved! So listen carefully to the answer,
the plain meaning of what is revealed."*
DANIEL 9:23 MSG

Graduation is an important milepost on your road map for
life. While you may or may not have plans for your future,
each day is full of decisions that will determine where you end
up tonight, tomorrow, and for the rest of your life.

Perhaps you've used Google Maps or MapQuest to plan a
trip. Isn't it great to have a visual of your route and to understand the twists, turns, and possible ways to reach your des-
tination? It prepares you for the journey by highlighting the
stops you should make, places you should rest, or locations
where you can fill your tank along the way.

Prayer works the same way for your spiritual journey.
Close communication with your heavenly Father provides you
with the direction, guidance, and provision you need to make
the right choices for every decision you face. *Power Prayers
for the Graduate* will help you discover the power of prayer,
understand the character and nature of God, and realize the
difference God's Word can make in your life every moment,
every day.

The Bible gives us wonderful examples of how God heard
the prayers of His people and how He answered those prayers
in life-changing ways. Take the story of Nehemiah, one of the
Bible's most adaptable and creative heroes. Devoted to a life of
prayer, Nehemiah lived to do God's will.

A young Jew from a prominent family during the Babylonian captivity, Nehemiah served as cupbearer to the Persian king, Artaxerxes. In Nehemiah's day, kings required someone to test any liquid before they drank it to ensure the king would not be poisoned. Nehemiah was considered loyal, and his duties gave him opportunity to talk with the king.

Nehemiah's brother brought him devastating news about his people back in Jerusalem: "Those who survived the exile and are back in the province are in great trouble and disgrace. The wall of Jerusalem is broken down, and its gates have been burned with fire" (Nehemiah 1:3).

Israel's enemies had attacked Nehemiah's homeland, broken its walls, and burned its gates. Nehemiah realized his people were unable to rebuild or repair the wall of Jerusalem. The news made him heartsick because of his intense love for his land and his burning passion to see his people established once again in the position of power the Lord had promised them.

Nehemiah mourned his people's losses, fasted, and then he prayed. He started with praise and worship, reminding himself of who God is and what He had done for him and for His people. He continued by taking responsibility for his wrong actions and those of his people, asking for forgiveness for himself and them (Nehemiah 1:6–7). Nehemiah then reminded God of His promise to bring Israel together again. He asked God to give him favor with the king so Artaxerxes would grant him permission to return to Jerusalem to restore the wall and the city's defenses.

God was faithful to Nehemiah and answered his prayer. In pursuit of his passion, Nehemiah traveled to Jerusalem to fulfill his dream.

Perhaps there are things in your life you are pursuing with passion. Have you invited God to participate? Maybe you need to start where Nehemiah did, by remembering who God is and what He's done in your life so far.

After you've praised God, do you need to confess anything to Him? What is keeping you from pursuing your dream? Are there things you know shouldn't be in your life—bad habits you want to break, relationships that have tied you to the wrong crowd, or hidden hurts you can't seem to forgive? All of us want positive change in our lives, but we often feel we don't have the power to make change happen.

Finally, are you willing to ask God to help you? Sometimes we think God isn't concerned about the little things—where you work or what classes you take, who you date, or even where you eat dinner. A story like Nehemiah's could make you think God concerns Himself only with bigger issues, but what's important to you is also important to Him.

Above all else—God desires a relationship with you. Prayer opens the door to relationship, but you have to invite Him in. God wants a relationship with all of humankind—He created us in His own image so we could become an expression of who He is (Genesis 1:26).

Prayer is an amazing exchange with God Almighty, talking and listening to the One who knows you better than you know yourself and loves you more than you can understand. He alone has the power to transform you and make lasting changes in your life.

Maybe you talk to God regularly, but you feel you can't quite reach Him. Does your time in prayer feel boring—does your mind wander? Maybe you're too busy—the desire to spend time with God is there, but your schedule is full, or all the things you have to do have caused you to be distracted. There's hope! It's time to put power in your prayers.

How to Use This Book

Power Prayers for the Graduate can help you get started. The prayers are written specifically to help you get to know your heavenly Father and His Word. As you allow the Holy Spirit to make scripture alive in your heart and mind, you will begin to know God personally. That's what Jesus meant when He said, "The words I say to you are not just my own. Rather, it is the Father, living in me, who is doing his work" (John 14:10).

Each chapter of this book contains a brief overview of an important prayer focus—topics such as friends and family, finances, dreams, fears, and your future. The chapter overview sets the scene to help you explore your circumstances and what God has to say about matters that are important to Him and to you.

Each chapter also gives you specific prayers on various topics that you can use "as is" or as starter prayers—simple prayers to which you can add your own words as you continue praying. Most importantly, many of these prayers come from scripture, so you'll be praying the Word—what God says about what concerns you. It's the most powerful way to pray!

God is an audience of One, available throughout the day and night for a constant exchange of worship, praise, thanksgiving, or for simply enjoying His presence as you would the company of a good friend. Prayer exists in those powerful moments when you honestly and openly express to God who you are—and who God is to you.

Allow your times of prayer to guide you on your spiritual journey. Stay connected to your heavenly Father—the source of direction you need for a successful life. As you begin your journey, read each topic slowly and allow time for your heart to soak up the Word. Then listen for the Holy Spirit to nudge you toward the right answers for your life.

Lord, I want to know You. I want to experience
Your presence in a more real way than ever before. I want to
hear Your voice and follow You all the days of my life. My heart
cries to know You more. Teach me Your truths and write
them upon my heart so I may understand who
You are and who You created me to be.

My Bible

The Power of God's Words

You can probably name several people who have some kind of power in your life. As a student, you have to obey the rules your teachers enforce. As a licensed driver, you have to follow traffic laws or face the consequences. As an employee, you have to please your boss, who has the power to hire and fire, promote and demote. Like it or not, your parents have the power to make decisions for your life until you turn eighteen. These people hold the power—granting permission for you to do certain things.

You also allow people you admire and respect to speak to you with some authority. You value their opinions and weigh their words as you make life decisions.

The Bible consists of God's words, the ultimate authority and power for your life. It's not just a reference book filled with stories of the past; it contains promises from God for your life. "The word of God is living and active. Sharper than any double-edged sword, it penetrates even to dividing soul and spirit, joints and marrow; it judges the thoughts and attitudes of the heart" (Hebrews 4:12).

When an *American Idol* finalist steps on stage, you expect to hear an amazing voice filled with power and talent. Imagine the sound all of heaven heard when God spoke the worlds into existence. His words created Earth and everything in it.

He called light to be and the oceans to divide. He formed every living thing with the sound of His voice (Genesis 1, Hebrews 11:3). His words commanded creation to happen with unimaginable power.

Now think about your Bible. It is full of God's words—scriptures inspired by God (2 Timothy 3:16). God created the world with words—and it is His Word that you can hold in your hand.

As you study your Bible and learn what God has to say about your life, allow your heart to become full of truth and life. You'll come to know God and His answers to the questions you face every day. You learn how to have a personal relationship with God by knowing Him through His Word, speaking to Him when you pray, and then listening to His voice as He speaks to you.

Jesus used scripture after a time of prayer and fasting when He was tempted by the devil: "Then Jesus, being filled with the Holy Spirit, returned from the Jordan and was led by the Spirit into the wilderness, being tempted for forty days by the devil. And in those days He ate nothing, and afterward, when they had ended, He was hungry. And the devil said to Him, 'If You are the Son of God, command this stone to become bread.' But Jesus answered him, saying, 'It is written, Man shall not live by bread alone, but by every word of God'" (Luke 4:1–4 NKJV).

Jesus knew the Bible. He knew His Father's opinion on the situation, and He overcame the devil with the power of the Word and prayer.

As you pray, remember the power His Word has in your life. When you pray according to God's will, you have all of heaven backing you up.

Devoted to God's Word

Today I choose Your Word, Lord. Your way is just and right. I will take the path You have chosen for me, and I will walk in the direction Your Word tells me to go. Help me to follow You with all my heart. Help me to keep my heart right so I always do what pleases You. Help me to keep Your commandments. Show me biblical truths. I am devoted to Your Word. I take it to heart so I will not sin against You.

The Way of Truth

Lord, give me understanding so I can know You better. Help me to keep Your commandments and obey Your truth with all my heart. I want to become passionate about Your Word. Turn my heart toward Your desires for my life. In Your truth I find comfort and peace. Turn my eyes away from worthless things and keep my focus on You. Your truth speaks clearly to me every day, so I can live my life according to Your will.

How I long for your precepts!
Preserve my life in your righteousness.
PSALM 119:40

Life for Your Soul

Your Word is perfect, Your principles long-standing and proven over many lifetimes. You revive my soul with Your wise and trustworthy commands. Your Word fills my heart with joy. Lord, help me to realize my mistakes, and please forgive my hidden sins. May the words of my mouth and the meditation of my heart be pleasing in Your sight. You steady me in troubled times with the truth of Your Word (Psalm 19:7–11).

To Understand the Bible

Scripture promises that I can have the mind of Christ so I can know and understand Your words. God, direct my heart and mind as I study and pray. Show me the things I need to comprehend. Make Your wisdom known to me. Help my heart and mind to be fixed on You. Give me great joy in discovering who I am in Christ and the plan You have for my life.

Study to shew thyself approved unto God,
a workman that needeth not to be ashamed,
rightly dividing the word of truth.
2 TIMOTHY 2:15 KJV

According to God's Will

Lord, I want to please You and do Your will all the days of my life. Forgive me when my own desires rise to the surface. I know that You hear my prayers and that Your Word is active and living in me. I stand on the promises I read in the Bible. Set my feet firmly on Your truth. I am rooted, grounded, and determined to live by faith and do what You want me to do. I will speak Your Word boldly and courageously today.

Power of the Word

God, I believe Your Word is true, but sometimes I have a hard time acting on it and following through with what I know is right. Help me to stand on Your promises. You have put Your power behind Your Word, and I trust You to do what You have promised.

> *Therefore, we never stop thanking God that when you received*
> *his message from us, you didn't think of our words as*
> *mere human ideas. You accepted what we said as the very*
> *word of God—which, of course, it is. And this word*
> *continues to work in you who believe.*
> 1 THESSALONIANS 2:13 NLT

Water the Word

As I study the Bible, the seeds of Your Word are planted in my heart. I pray that Your truths deepen in me. Just as a tree grows strong planted by a river filled with good nutrients, I grow stronger each day through the water of Your Word. I will never fail because Your Word lives in me and Your Word will never fail. When I gave my life to You, Lord, You started a good work in me, and I know that it will continue until You return.

Guided by Truth

I trust You, Lord, with all my heart. In everything I do, I acknowledge You and give Your Word first place in my life. I walk in the light of Your Word, stepping where You shine the light of truth, trusting I am in the right place at the right time to live my life according to Your purposes. I refuse to veer to the right or the left, but take comfort knowing that You are always guiding me. I listen as Your voice speaks to me, showing me the way to go.

Integrity of the Word

Father, I have great respect for Your Word. I give it first place in my life. Your Word is my umpire, settling disputes and answering questions that I face every day. I refuse to compromise. I set my heart upon the foundation of Your Word and will not be moved from it.

"Do not let this Book of the Law depart from your mouth; meditate on it day and night, so that you may be careful to do everything written in it. Then you will be prosperous and successful."
JOSHUA 1:8

Limitless Power of God's Word

Thank You, God, for giving me Your Word—Your promise for all eternity. I choose to trust and believe Your Word above all else. I build my faith and hope on You and the power of Your Word. It is alive and working in my life. I know that when I speak Your truths and apply faith, Your Word will accomplish what You sent it to do in my life.

But Jesus looked at them and said to them, "With men this is impossible, but with God all things are possible."
MATTHEW 19:26 NKJV

The Power of Living in the Word

Lord, You gave Your Word to live in my heart. Father, please allow the seed of Your Word to grow mightily in me, filling me with the power and truth of all You created me to be. Your Word is a lamp to my feet and a light to my path, showing me the right way to live my life as a reflection of You on the earth.

Potential of God's Words

Lord, You have put Your desires in my heart and set me on Earth to fulfill Your purpose. You have promised that You will accomplish Your plan for my life. There is no word spoken by You that is ever powerless. Today I choose to believe Your Word. I stand strong, knowing that You will help me achieve my full potential as I hold fast to the truths in the Bible—Your living words for my life.

Demonstrate God's Word

Father, as I grow in Your Word, help me to show others the awesome power of Your Word. Let my life be an example of truth for the whole world to see. Help me to live my life before all people, demonstrating the faithfulness of Your promises found in the Bible. Show people through me that You are genuine, real, and true to Your Word.

By faith we understand that the worlds were framed by the
word of God, so that the things which are seen were
not made of things which are visible.
HEBREWS 11:3 NKJV

Answers in the Bible

Lord, when I feel lost and far from You, help me to find comfort in Your Word. Let Your words speak to me as though You were whispering encouragement and direction into my ear. Hold me up with the power of Your Word when I feel defeated. Give me strength when I feel drained by the pressures of my circumstances. Direct my eyes to the scriptures You want me to read for the answers I need today. You know what I need even before I ask.

My Faith

The Power of Knowing God

How many times have you taken a seat in class, plopped down on a couch, or leaned back in a recliner without a second thought as to whether the furniture would hold you? You had no expectation of it letting you hit the ground unless you'd had an experience of falling. Then you might second-guess your faith in that chair, couch, or recliner.

Faith in what we can see is easy for us. We live in a natural world, and we rely on our five senses to tell us what to expect from the things we do each day. We expect the engine in our car to start when we turn the key. We expect our tires to hold air, and we trust that other drivers will obey the traffic lights and road signs.

The natural can fail us, and does. Yet while we see accidents on the road every day because others fail to obey the law, we still expect to come and go each day safely.

Our faith in the unseen should be even stronger. Spiritually we should have an even higher expectation to see fulfilled the promises God has made to us; and yet we don't always believe we will receive results when we pray.

Jesus said, "I tell you, you can pray for anything, and if you believe that you've received it, it will be yours." (Mark 11:24 NLT). That promise is from Jesus Christ Himself. Yet day after day we find ourselves doubting because we can't see the fulfillment of our requests.

How many times have you given up on what you've asked God for because you didn't see it in the time frame you expected? God doesn't work on our timetables. Sometimes it takes time, effort, and energy to move circumstances out of the way in order to make a clear path for the things we ask for, much like moving a physical mountain into the sea.

Imagine you were in a park and you threw a Frisbee. You waited for it to come back, but then you became discouraged, disappointed, or distracted, left the park, and went home. Imagine the next day the Frisbee came back but you were gone.

When you give up waiting for the answer to your prayer request, it's as though you stopped watching for God to throw a Frisbee back. The answer to your prayer is coming back to you, but you're gone. You never waited to receive it.

God does what He does in His own time. You have to be patient and keep believing that He's working behind the scenes to bring answers for your life. He wants to give you the desires of your heart when you pray according to His purposes and plan. Don't quit believing. Keep expecting to receive what you asked for.

Praise for God's Indescribable Gift

Thank You for giving the most precious gift, Your very own Son, so I could live each day with You. There are no words to describe the depths of Your sacrifice, but I know You did it for me. You gave Your first and only Son so You could share life with many sons and daughters. I am so thankful Jesus was willing to give His life for mine.

"For God so loved the world that he gave his one and only Son, that whoever believes in him shall not perish but have eternal life."
JOHN 3:16

Your Gift Accepted

Jesus, please be the Lord and Savior of my life. I confess my sins to You. Take my life and purge me from all that is ungodly and of this world. Fill me with new life. Make me a new creature, filled with Your Spirit. I willingly give You my life—take it and make it whatever pleases You. Without You I am nothing, but in You I can reach my full potential. Help me to live my life so that I am a reflection of You, pointing others to eternal life with You.

The Fullness of the Holy Spirit

Thank You, Lord, for Your Holy Spirit. I trust that the Holy Spirit leads and guides me in every area of my life. You sent the Holy Spirit to comfort me and teach me all things. He directs my steps and helps me to make wise life choices. He shows me God's best for my life. I set my heart on the promise of His presence and diligently listen to His leading.

Do not get drunk on wine, which leads to debauchery.
Instead, be filled with the Spirit.
EPHESIANS 5:18

Knowing God Is There

God, I know You are there. Even though I can't see You with my eyes, I sense Your presence when I pray. When I feel alone, I remember Your promise to never leave me. Faith allows me to see the unseen, to trust what I cannot touch. I rely on my spiritual senses to get me through to the other side of the challenges in my life—the challenges that tempt me to doubt You and let go of the truth of Your love. Thank You for always making Yourself known to me when I need You.

Take Up Your Cross

Jesus, it takes sacrifice to follow You. I have so many dreams for my life, but they are nothing unless they include You. Help me to let go of the things I selfishly desire and that aren't meant to be a part of my life. Your purposes for my life mean success. I give You my life—I completely surrender.

> *Then he said to the crowd, "If any of you wants to be my follower, you must turn from your selfish ways, take up your cross daily, and follow me."*
> LUKE 9:23 NLT

Finding Faith

Father, the Bible says every person has been given a measure of faith. I already have faith—You instilled it in me when I gave my life to You. Sometimes I don't feel as if I have much faith, especially when I wonder how You could possibly turn my messy life around. But You are always faithful, and I have to remember all You have already brought me through. Help me to grow in faith. Help me to remember that the more I trust You while facing difficulty, the stronger my faith becomes.

Asking for God's Help

Sometimes I feel You have so much on Your plate that I should work things out on my own. I know I shouldn't feel like I'm bothering You, but my problems seem small compared to what others deal with. Still, I know You want to help me. You are just waiting for me to ask, so I'm asking—please, help. You know what I'm dealing with. Forgive me for not coming to You sooner. I accept Your help today.

God is my helper; the Lord is with those who uphold my life.
PSALM 54:4 NKJV

Knowing God's Mercy

Father, You love me with no strings attached. No matter what I do or don't do, You show me grace that makes me love You more. Everywhere I turn, Your eyes are on me, caring for me with a compassion greater than the love I could ever experience from anyone else. Thank You for Your promise that Your mercy follows me all the days of my life.

For the LORD your God is a merciful God; he will not abandon
or destroy you or forget the covenant with your forefathers,
which he confirmed to them by oath.
DEUTERONOMY 4:31

Seeing the Unseen

Lord, I am learning so much. I want to see You in the small moments in my life today. I don't want to take anything for granted, so show me the majestic beauty of Your creation. I want to experience You in all I see. Help me to see the unseen. Give me wisdom to read and understand Your Word. Give me discernment so I know the right things I should do. Open the eyes of my spirit so I can see clearly from Your perspective.

The Power of God's Protection

Fairy tales and fables always have a hero—a rescuer, protector, and conqueror. God, You created me and gave me life. You are the One who saves my life every day. You have given Your angels charge over me to keep me protected. You go before me and fight my battles, sometimes without me ever knowing those battles exist. You are my refuge and my shield. Thank You for always being there.

> *"For the LORD your God is He who goes with you,*
> *to fight for you against your enemies, to save you."*
> DEUTERONOMY 20:4 NKJV

Increase My Faith

Jesus, You promised if I believe when I pray according to our Father's will, then I can have what I ask. It's so hard to believe sometimes, especially when it seems my prayer is taking a long time to be answered. Forgive me for not trusting You. You have never failed me, and sometimes I forget that. Help me to stand in faith, knowing that I will see the results of my faith. Remind me that answers come in Your time, not mine. You are the finisher of my faith, so I hold tight to You.

The Power of God's Closeness

God, I am depending on my own abilities. I don't want to feel far from You, but I do. Yet being close to You is more than a feeling. As I draw closer to You, I know You will draw closer to me. Your presence gives me an inner strength that is not my own. Let me experience You as if You were standing close enough that I could feel Your breath on my face.

What other great nation has gods that are intimate with them the way GOD, our God, is with us, always ready to listen to us?
DEUTERONOMY 4:7 MSG

Experiencing God's Strength

Life's demands seem heavier than ever before. I am taking a moment right now to recharge my soul with Your strength. Remind me that my help comes from You—whatever I need. You are my power source, and I plug in right now. Fill me up physically, mentally, and emotionally. Thank You that I don't have to go through my life alone. You are always there to recharge me when my power supply is running low. I rest in You today.

> *God is my strength and power,*
> *and He makes my way perfect.*
> 2 SAMUEL 22:33 NKJV

Praying God's Words

I don't have to worry about my problems today. You are giving me the answers I need to change my life. Hebrews 4:12 says Your Word is alive and active, sharper than a double-edged sword. When I speak and pray the scriptures, I am agreeing with You in what You want to do on the earth and in my life. I attach my faith to Your words, and You give life to the desires of my heart. As I pray today, I know Your power is released to answer my prayers.

My Identity

The Power of Who I Am in Christ

One recent graduate, who had not yet decided if she was ready to hit the job market, prepared for the onslaught of questions for back-to-school night at her daughter's elementary school. She had cleverly ordered business cards that read: JULIE STOUT, DOMESTIC ENGINEER, with her home phone and address, cell phone, and e-mail address.

The way we think of ourselves has everything to do with how the world sees us. When you look in the mirror, you see a graduate—but what kind of graduate? Are you confident, shy, easily intimidated, or ready to take on the world? *Graduate* doesn't really tell the world who you are, but it does say that you are transitioning to the next step in your life.

When you meet someone, the first question you're asked after your name is, "What do you do?" We define each other by what we *do* rather than who we *are*. Often our occupations, instead of our commitment to Christ, define us to others.

Jesus asked His disciples, "Who do men say that I am?" The disciples replied from various people's perspectives, "John the Baptist; but some say, Elijah; and others, one of the prophets." Then Jesus pointed the question at them, "But who do you say that I am?" Peter answered, "You are the Christ" (Mark 8:27–29).

Peter recognized Jesus because the Holy Spirit revealed

who He was. Through the Holy Spirit's revelation, the disciples saw God when they saw Jesus. He said and did what the Father told Him to do and say. He lived in the power of His heavenly Father's will, consistent with His Father's character.

At some point in your life you were probably introduced to someone based on your relationship with someone else—Annie's sister, Professor Vance's student, or Rich's friend. Now, imagine if you were introduced to others based on your relationship with God. *This is God's child, Stephen. He's the spitting image of his heavenly Father—so strong and courageous.* Or, *C'mon over and meet Shelley, she's so compassionate, just like Christ!*

As a Christian, your relationship with God should be the foundation of your identity. The only way to find out who you are and who you are meant to be is to discover God's identity and the character that goes along with it.

Ephesians 5:1 says, "Be imitators of God, therefore, as dearly loved children."

Throughout the Bible you read of who God is and how He relates to you. You can find your own identity within the pages that describe His character, His morals, His values, His work ethic—His identity. As you spend time in prayer with Him, you will experience His presence and a personal relationship with Him, and you will grow in His likeness.

The amazing power of who you are in Christ provides you with everything you need to succeed. When you are weak, He is strong. He has made you more than a conqueror, an overcomer in this life. No matter what battles you face, you can do all things through Christ who gives you strength.

I Am God's Child

Jesus, thank You for providing the way for me to belong to Your family. Everyone who accepts You and believes in You becomes a child of God. I am born of God—not from natural birth, but spiritual birth. You are my example, and I will do my best to follow in Your footsteps. I want to be like You and our heavenly Father. I want to have the same character and nature. I receive Your gift of inclusion in the greatest family of all eternity.

The Spirit of God, who raised Jesus from the dead, lives in you.
ROMANS 8:11 NLT

God's Definition

When I meet new people, they always ask me what I do. Then I feel as though they're judging me as to whether I should be remembered. It's hard *not* to allow what I do to define me. Help me remember that my education and profession don't define me. Even who my parents are and where I grew up or went to school have nothing to do with who You created me to be. You are the Creator and, therefore, You define me. You make me who I am created to be. I am Your child, committed to living a life as genuine and true to Your purpose and plan as I can.

A Matter of Significance

Jesus, help me to find my identity in You. I know that my relationship with You is significant. As I read the Bible, give me an understanding of who You created me to be. Point out the true identity that has been given to me through the gift of salvation and my relationship with You.

To them God willed to make known what are the riches of
the glory of this mystery among the Gentiles:
which is Christ in you, the hope of glory.
COLOSSIANS 1:27 NKJV

Facing the Truth

Lord, I know I need to change a lot of things in my life. Thank You for accepting me as I am, where I am today. You see the potential of who I can be, even when I can't see it. Show me the things in my heart that You want to change. Open my eyes; I don't want to pretend anymore. Help me see the truth so You can make me new!

The spirit of a man is the lamp of the LORD, searching all the inner depths of his heart.
PROVERBS 20:27 NKJV

A Vote of Confidence

I don't want to pretend to be someone I'm not. Help me to stand up to the pressure that others place on me to conform. Lord, You are my confidence! I can do all things through Jesus Christ who gives me strength to face today's challenges—even when those challenges are people. Give me the words to stay true to my commitment to You. I remind myself of all the things that You have done, all the battles You have fought on my behalf. With You at my side and in my heart, I know I can succeed.

An Imitator of God

Father, my relationship with You affects my personality in amazing ways. Many people have a negative idea of what it means to be a Christian. Forgive me when I've failed to be like You. I want to be so full of Your presence that others see You in everything I say and do. I never want anything I do to reflect negatively on You. I want to be like Jesus, of whom people said, "This truly was the Son of God!"

> *Everyone who believes that Jesus is the Christ*
> *has become a child of God.*
> 1 JOHN 5:1 NLT

Finding Courage

Jesus, thank You for the courage to live my life following Your example. I can do all things through You who gives me the power to succeed. I refuse to be intimidated by what others say, think, or do. I live my life according to our Father's will and the Holy Spirit's instruction. Help me to declare to others the freedom I have found in You, so I point the way to You. Equip me to lead others to follow You.

Finding Assurance

When people see me, let them see You. Help me not to confuse who You say I am with self-confidence, arrogance, or pride. My confidence is only because You live in and through me. Give me wisdom to know when to speak and when to listen so others may know You through my actions.

*I have been crucified with Christ and I no longer live,
but Christ lives in me. The life I live in the body, I live by faith
in the Son of God, who loved me and gave himself for me.*
GALATIANS 2:20

Living without Guilt or Shame

I have a list of things that make me feel guilty. They shout at me. I've told You my sins, and You have forgiven me, but I remember. Lord, help me to let go of my past mistakes. Help me to forgive myself. These things are like heavy chains keeping me from living the life of freedom that comes from a relationship with You. Today, I lift them off my shoulders and leave them at Your feet. Help me to never pick them up again. I let them go now. I am free today in Jesus' name!

Life from a Positive Perspective

As I learn who I am in Christ, I realize that I need to look at life from a positive perspective. My life in You is not about what I'm missing or don't have. It's about Your light and life working in and through me. In even the most difficult situations I will find Your goodness in me.

But you are a chosen people, a royal priesthood, a holy nation, a people belonging to God, that you may declare the praises of him who called you out of darkness into his wonderful light.
1 PETER 2:9

Nothing Missing — Complete

I always felt I was missing something in my life before I met You. You are the missing piece of the puzzle. Now, no matter what I face I know that I lack no good thing. When I am weak, You are strong. Instead of discouragement, I have boldness to do the things that without You I couldn't do. When life is a mess, You comfort me with Your peace. With You in my life, I am complete. All I need is You—nothing else.

To Live in Christ

In Your love and mercy You gave me life when You raised Christ from the dead. I was lost and alone, but You found me. You picked me up and gave me all the benefits of Your own Son, Jesus. Thank You for Your incredible kindness. All I had to do was believe and receive this gift. I can't take credit for it—it was all You! Father, continue to make me new each day in Christ.

Anyone who belongs to Christ has become a new person.
The old life is gone; a new life has begun!
2 CORINTHIANS 5:17 NLT

To Be a Peacemaker

Jesus, You said, "Blessed are the peacemakers, for they will be called sons of God" (Matthew 5:9). I want to be a peacemaker because it brings me closer to You. Help me to be open to other points of view and to think before I talk. Show me Your plan of peace in difficult situations. Remind me that it's more important to let others see You in me than to prove to them that I am right. When there doesn't seem to be a peaceful solution, show me Your way to peace.

Let Love Rule

Lord, help me to get rid of anger, cruelty, slander, and dirty language. I have the mind of Christ and can exercise self-control. Show me how to live my life with mercy, kindness, humility, gentleness, and patience. Remind me to allow for others' faults, even when they don't allow for mine. I want to be quick to forgive. Above all, help me to let Christ govern my heart. Please forgive me when I forget and take control.

> *"Live out your God-created identity. Live generously and graciously toward others, the way God lives toward you."*
> MATTHEW 5:48 MSG

My Friends

The Power of Lasting Connections

When you meet persons you feel you've known all your life, it's easy to open up, take off your mask, and let them experience the *real* you. You're comfortable with them, and it's easy to share your life with them. A good friend is one of the greatest treasures you'll find.

As you prepared to graduate, you and your school friends probably spent time reminding each other of all the funny stories and great times you shared together. Maybe it's a little sad to realize each of you will go your own way as you enter the next step in your journey toward the destiny God has for you.

God made us to thrive as social beings, and the exchange between friends is essential. Friends offer love, support, and companionship. Because friends give advice and have a strong influence, you must choose them very carefully. A true friend provides wise counsel, encouragement, and unconditional love.

Those friends closest to you encourage you to be yourself at all times. You don't have to be on guard because you know they won't misjudge or hurt you. You can laugh, cry, and safely share the deepest secrets of your soul with a true friend.

Now, friendship isn't easy—it's the rough times that you go through together that connect your souls together. It takes courage to share yourself, effort to take risks and commit to each other.

An amazing story of friendship unfolded in 1 and 2 Samuel. David and Jonathan swore their loyalty to one another. "Now when he had finished speaking to Saul, the soul of Jonathan was knit to the soul of David, and Jonathan loved him as his own soul. Saul took him that day, and would not let him go home to his father's house anymore. Then Jonathan and David made a covenant, because he loved him as his own soul" (1 Samuel 18:1–3 NKJV).

They remained loyal to each other, although their friendship was challenged by daunting obstacles. Jonathan's father, King Saul, chased after David to kill him because David had been appointed the next king of Israel by the prophet Samuel. Jonathan risked his father's enmity by helping David.

God has divine connections for your life—people who will help you grow in Christ and support you as together you strive to accomplish the plan God has for you. Every person you meet adds to or subtracts from your life. It's important to fill your time with the right people.

Ask God to direct you in your relationships. Examine them. Are there unhealthy relationships that need to be severed? Ask Him to show you how to do that.

As you apply God's wisdom to your life and spend time with people He's brought into your life, your friendships will become for a season or a lifetime the healthy, two-way commitments that mark balanced relationships.

Thanks for My Friends

Thank You, Lord, for my friends. I appreciate that they accept me for who I am and encourage me to grow in my relationship with You. They want to see me succeed in every area of my life. They are there for me when I need them, concerned for my life just as I am for theirs. Thank You for the courage to be open and truthful with them. You have joined our hearts together with Your love.

> *The soul of Jonathan was knit to the soul of David,*
> *and Jonathan loved him as his own soul.*
> 1 SAMUEL 18:1 NKJV

To Be a Better Friend

Father, help me to be sensitive to the people around me. When I am tempted to make things all about me, remind me that You created me for friendship. I want to be a better friend. Help me to prefer others to myself. I want to be a better listener so I really hear my friends. I want to help them if I can in the things that concern them. Let my words encourage them. Show me how to strengthen them with Your goodness.

Choosing Friends Wisely

Your Word says two are better than one, because if one falls, there will be someone to lift that person up. Lord, I ask for divine connections, good friends only You can give. Help me to let go of relationships that are unhealthy and negative. I want friends who speak and live positively, who inspire and encourage but also tell me the truth when I need to hear it. Give me wisdom today in the relationships I choose.

> *The godly give good advice to their friends;*
> *the wicked lead them astray.*
> PROVERBS 12:26 NLT

When Friendships Fail

I'm hurt, angry, and finding it difficult to forgive. I thought my friend and I would be there for each other forever. Help me to handle feelings of rejection. Help me to forgive, and if it's Your will for this person to be in my life, then help us to be reconciled to each other so we can share our lives again. And if not, show me how to move forward without my friend.

Hurt by a Friend

Lord, I feel I opened my heart to my friend and it was stomped on. I'm so hurt. Whether my friend did it on purpose or not, the pain is the same. And I'm supposed to forgive? I don't know what to say. I need a little time to distance myself from what happened. Help me to find the words to express my feelings, and please do a work in my heart so I can let go of the pain and forgive.

> *Love prospers when a fault is forgiven,*
> *but dwelling on it separates close friends.*
> PROVERBS 17:9 NLT

A Firmly Founded Friendship

I want to do what it takes to build lasting friendships with people You have put in my life, Lord. My friends are important to me. Yet life is busy, and sometimes I put the things I need to do to get ahead before my relationships. Lord, help me to establish a firm foundation of loyalty, trust, honesty, and integrity in my friendships. When our eyes are on You, we will remain strong in our commitment to You and to one another. Help me to discern when I need to drop a task and be there for my friends.

Truthful Friendship

The Bible says that as iron sharpens iron, so true friends sharpen the hearts and minds of one another. God, I want to have relationships that are true and honest. Help me to tell the truth in the most gentle and positive way. I want my friends to know the truth about me and about the things that concern them. When they ask my advice, help me to share truth and wisdom from You that will help them grow in their relationship with You. Show them that I love them and want Your best for their lives.

The godly give good advice to their friends;
the wicked lead them astray.
PROVERBS 12:26 NLT

To Look to the Heart

You know the hearts of everyone, Lord. At first glance, all I see is outward appearances. I want to be a good judge of character. Help me to be discerning. Make me aware when I am being negatively influenced or manipulated. Teach me what I need to know to be a quality friend, and show me the hearts of my friends.

> *As for those who seemed to be important—*
> *whatever they were makes no difference to me;*
> *God does not judge by external appearance.*
> GALATIANS 2:6

Pleasing God instead of People

Lord, help me to make friends with people who like me for me. Don't let me fall into the trap of trying to win friends by doing things that will entertain or please them. Help me to be a leader and not a follower. The only One I want to please is You. Give me courage when I find myself in the wrong crowd. Help me stay balanced in my friendships, so I will always seek to please You rather than other people.

In the Face of Prejudice

All men and women are equal in Your sight. Jesus died for every one of us, no matter where we come from or what color our skin is. Help me not to value one relationship over another because of influence, wealth, intellect, or race. Help me to see others from Your perspective, no matter how different other people are from me. Help me to love them and learn from the differences we have.

Therefore, accept each other just as Christ has
accepted you so that God will be given glory.
ROMANS 15:7 NLT

To Be There for Others

Thank You, Lord, for the rich blessings You have given me in my understanding friends. No matter what challenges we face, we face them together. Help me always to be there for them. No matter what they are facing, give me the patience to stand with them, no matter how long it takes. Even when things that concern them don't seem all that important to me, remind me that they would be there for me if I needed them. Help me to remember them in my prayers, and remind me that my relationships with them are centered in our faith in You.

Pure Motives

Lord, help me to examine my motives in pursuit of friendship. Why do I seek relationships with certain people? Give me the courage to look truthfully into my heart and see my true intentions. Sometimes I think a relationship with a certain person might help me look better in the eyes of others. I am ambitious, but I know it's wrong to use people to get what I want. You supply everything I need. Help me to maintain right and pure relationships before You.

To flatter friends is to lay a trap for their feet.
PROVERBS 29:5 NLT

On Graduation Day

Here we are, Lord, on Graduation Day. Thank You for helping me get this far. Help me to step out in faith and pursue the dream You have given me. Direct my path so I don't lose contact with friends. Give me wisdom in the choices I'll make after today. I pray for my classmates, that each one of them will know You and live a life pleasing to You. Keep them from harm and give them the desires of their hearts.

Opposite-Sex Friendships

Heavenly Father, I have a great friend of the opposite gender. I ask You to help me to be a real friend and to consider my motives. I never want to take advantage of my friend in any way. Help me always to be up front with my feelings. If I ever start feeling attracted to my friend, show me how to let this person know, and help us to count the cost before we change our relationship in any way.

> *He who walks with wise men will be wise,*
> *but the companion of fools will suffer harm.*
> PROVERBS 13:20 NASB

My Family

The Power of Relationship

Families of students come together to celebrate at graduation ceremonies. During graduation you experience cameras flashing, proud parents pointing and crying, and cheers from family and friends as grads cross the stage.

If you look across the sea of people at events like that, you quickly realize families can take various shapes—grandparents raising grandchildren, single moms and dads, and siblings raising younger siblings.

No matter what your family looks like, God purposefully placed you in a family. Family is a God idea. He puts people on the earth through families. "I will bless [Sarah] and will surely give you a son by her. I will bless her so that she will be the mother of nations; kings of peoples will come from her" (Genesis 17:16).

Whether you've lived at home up until now or you've been on your own for a while, changes in your life and the lives of your family members bring challenge and an opportunity to grow together. Daily sharing our lives with one another helps us discover how to live successfully with those we love. A positive family environment offers laughter, hope, and unconditional love.

Home should be the one place where you feel safe and protected from the hard things the world throws at you. There are the memories, stories, and laughter you shared with your family. There are the times when you struggled and then hopefully grew closer. Maybe you were there for each other in all the time you spent together, all the challenges you faced, and achievements you celebrated.

Or maybe you weren't! Sometimes relationships are strained and families break. Trust is broken. God wants to heal those relationships and restore those wounded hearts. Prayer is the first place to start with your relationship with your family members.

Joseph's ten older brothers sold him into slavery. He was their father's favorite, and in their jealousy and anger they decided they should kill him. God spared Joseph from their wrath when one of the brothers convinced the rest of them to sell him into slavery instead.

Joseph's story, told in Genesis 37, is an amazing one of provision and forgiveness. God used a boy sold into slavery to save a nation—including Joseph's own father and brothers—from famine and death.

You and your family are important to God. Adam and Eve were created from His desire to have a big family of His own. He wanted to be a Father with a loving relationship with many sons and daughters. When Adam and Eve disobeyed God, sin separated Him from His family for what could have been eternity. He sent Jesus, His only Son, to give everyone the opportunity to be reunited with Him. Through your acceptance of Jesus Christ, you became a child of God and a member of His amazing family for all eternity.

No matter where you go, you are always a part of an eternal family.

For My Parents

Father, bless my parents. They have raised me the best way they know how. As I've grown up, there have been times when I thought I was smarter than they were, or that they just didn't understand me. Forgive me for the things I did that may have hurt them. I was trying to find my place as an adult. Draw us closer together and help us enjoy our friendship.

> *Pay close attention, friend, to what your father tells you;*
> *never forget what you learned at your mother's knee.*
> PROVERBS 1:8 MSG

When I've Hurt My Family

I've made decisions in my life that hurt my family. I didn't mean to hurt them. Please forgive me, and I pray they find it in their hearts to forgive me, too. I know they may never understand—please let that be okay. Heal our hurts for the words we've said to one another. Help us to better understand one another. Help them understand that I have to go my own way—even if that means making my own mistakes. Restore our relationship and open doors so that we can grow together again as a family.

Unsaved Loved Ones

It's been difficult serving You when my family members don't know You. I can't seem to make them understand. I don't want to argue or defend my relationship with You anymore. Help me to choose words and actions that let them see You in me. I pray they see the difference You have made in my life and that they'll come to know You, too.

Whenever we have the opportunity, we should do
good to everyone—especially to those in the family of faith.
GALATIANS 6:10 NLT

For My Future Spouse

Lord, help me to be a support to my future spouse. Help me to love this person unconditionally as Christ loves the church. Teach me how to meet my loved one's emotional, physical, and mental needs. I'll leave the spiritual needs to You. Draw my future spouse closer to You and help us to live our lives together focused on You. Teach us to pray together and rely on You in the decisions we make as a couple. Teach us to do life together as we follow after You.

Facing a Family Crisis

It is so hard dealing with this family crisis. Lord, teach me how to face these issues in a positive way. I feel so alone. Thank You for being with me. I can't be the one to fix this problem for them even though I'd like to. You're the only One who can. Bring people across my path whom I can talk to about this, people who can support me and lift me up. Help me to focus on what I have to do, and keep me from becoming distracted. I give it all to You right now. I know You won't let any of us down.

For the Children I Hope to Have

Heavenly Father, I thank You in advance for blessing my future spouse and me with children. We will treasure them as gifts from You. We will raise them to know You as a loving and good Father. We will teach them Your Word. I thank You that You will keep them healthy and whole every day of their lives. I thank You that they will have a personal relationship with You all their days. Fill them with Your presence and protect them, especially when I'm not with them.

I bow my knees to the Father of our Lord Jesus Christ, from whom the whole family in heaven and earth is named.
EPHESIANS 3:14–15 NKJV

For Peace in My Family

You have promised the peace that passes understanding. Thank You that Your Spirit lives in and with us. My family is blessed in all we do. I thank You, Lord, that Your peace goes with us. No matter how much chaos is going on around us, we can rest and rely on You. Help us not to get caught up in the moments when it seems the world is spinning out of control. Remind us to fix our minds and hearts on You and live in Your strength today.

Healing from Abuse

God, You know our history, where my family and I have come from. Thank You for bringing us into a place of safety. You have begun the healing of our hearts, minds, and emotions. Continue to fill us with Your mercy and love. Cover us with a blanket of assurance that the past is past. Help us to let go of painful memories and start life anew today.

They replied, "Believe in the Lord Jesus,
and you will be saved—you and your household."
ACTS 16:31

When a Loved One Dies

Father, I'm not grieving for the one who died, I'm grieving for myself. I will miss our special times together. My heart hurts and I can't believe they're gone. Sometimes I look up and think I'm going to see them standing there. Show me how to savor the memories we shared. Help my family and me grow closer to You through this sad time. My hope and expectation is in seeing my loved one again someday when You come and take us all to live with You.

For Stability in Relationships

Lord, I ask for You to stabilize my family relationships. Help us to overcome the things that cause us to push each other away. Teach us to be steady and strong for one another. Show us how we can honor each other. Soften our hearts and help us to forgive if we feel we've been wronged.

He is like a man building a house, who dug down deep and laid the foundation on rock. When a flood came, the torrent struck that house but could not shake it, because it was well built.
LUKE 6:48

When My Family Frustrates Me

God, I love my family members, but they frustrate me. I want to be there for them, and I want them to be there for me. But they make choices I don't understand. Instead of confronting them in anger, teach me how to pray for them and speak to them with Your love. Like me, they are still growing in their relationship with You and in their knowledge of Your Word. When conflicts arise, show me how to find solutions that benefit all of us according to Your purpose and Your plan for our family.

What to Say and Not Say

Father, my family member is hurting, going through a painful situation I don't understand. Help me to be supportive even when I have no understanding of what they're experiencing.

Bearing with one another, and forgiving one another,
if anyone has a complaint against another; even as Christ forgave
you, so you also must do. But above all these things put on love, which
is the bond of perfection. And let the peace of God rule in your hearts,
to which also you were called in one body; and be thankful.
COLOSSIANS 3:13–15 NKJV

A Fresh Start

I want a fresh start with my family. We've all made mistakes and disappointed one another in big and small ways. Help us to get past our faults and mistakes. Stop me when I'm tempted to bring up past stories that caused hurt, pain, or embarrassment. Remind us of the good times we all share. Help us to be caring and compassionate with one another. Give me the desire and ability to forgive the past, and help them to forgive me. Give us opportunities to make new memories as we grow in our relationships with You and each other.

For All Eternity

Lord, help me to recognize that eternity is now. We are eternal beings, and the things we do today are the beginning of forever. I want to spend eternity with my family members. Remind us that each day is a gift and that our time is precious. Help us not to waste it with idle words and quarreling. Thank You for giving us Your wisdom to make the most of every moment; to build each other up in faith.

As for me and my house, we will serve the LORD.
JOSHUA 24:15 NASB

My Fears

The Power of Trusting God

Fear disrupts your life, drains your strength, and clouds your judgment.

Perhaps you're struggling with the unknowns of your future or the fear of losing friendships or leaving family to pursue your dream. Maybe you fear failing at a career or making the right decision about continuing as a student. When you focus on your fears, you can become paralyzed, unable to achieve the things God put you on the earth to do.

God, your Creator, did not design you to have a spirit of fear, but a spirit of power, filled with love and complete soundness of mind (2 Timothy 1:7). The word *power* in this verse means *the inexhaustible strength that comes from God.*

The enemy of your soul—the devil—tries to deceive you into believing God is not all-powerful. John 10:10 gives you a clear picture of the devil's job description: "The thief comes only to steal and kill and destroy." Fear, his greatest tool, stands in opposition to your faith. The second half of John 10:10 tells us Jesus' purpose: "I have come that they may have life, and have it to the full."

God, through Jesus' resurrection, made a way for you to turn to Him during times when fear tries to take up residency in your heart. God is there *always*, and He wants you to draw strength and power from Him even in the midst of terrifying situations.

It's the ultimate ongoing battle: *Fear vs. Faith*! We struggle to believe the unseen God, trusting Him despite a lack of tangible assurances that all will work out well. The writer of Hebrews understood this: "Now faith is being sure of what we hope for and certain of what we do not see" (Hebrews 11:1). We can't *see* God, but we have examples in the Bible of the saints who lived by faith. We also draw insight from our connections with other people to better understand a trusting relationship with God.

Are you hesitant to put your confidence in God's promises because you're afraid you'll be disappointed?

Trust means depending on someone or something, especially in a time of crisis. It takes courage to trust God to fulfill His promises when we can't see Him acting on our behalf. Draw strength by thinking about the times you've trusted God. You may not have gotten the exact results you wanted, but He was always faithful to you. Remember the times you've reached out to Him and found Him there for you and consider each of them as a step up to the next level of trust. God promises to be with you every step of the way (Deuteronomy 31:6).

Learning to trust is important in your journey to a successful relationship with God and a successful life. What fears are you battling today? Write them down and give them to God in prayer.

Trusting God for Acceptance

When people laugh at me, I look to You. When they harass me, help me to be confident. In the midst of it all, remind me to praise You. Help me to be brave when my enemies threaten me. Lord, let Your kindness surround me, and bring me under the protection of those who love me because they love You. Teach me how to live confidently in who You created me to be.

> *"Anyone who trusts in him will never be put to shame."*
> ROMANS 10:11

Trusting God with Changes

Every day I feel the tug of transition. I know change enables me to grow and become who You created me to be. Help me to be willing to step out of my comfort zone to go where You want me to be. I want to remain focused on Your purpose for me, never looking back but pressing forward in my journey with You. Show me how to lean on You when I feel out of place or alone. I know You are always with me.

Trusting God for Safety

Father, I follow hard after You. I will not be distracted but choose to be at the right place at the right time, every time. Thank You for keeping me safe today. I am secure because You have made Your angels responsible to protect me at all times. Disasters are far from me because I walk on the path of safety.

> *"In righteousness you will be established: Tyranny will be far*
> *from you; you will have nothing to fear. Terror will be*
> *far removed; it will not come near you."*
> ISAIAH 54:14

Peace for Today

Jesus, thank You for the peace that You give me daily. Because You have promised me peace, I refuse to be worried about things I don't have answers for right now. You know what I need to know. Thank You for the Holy Spirit You have given to encourage and guide me. He makes the hidden things known when I need to know them. I rely on Him to teach me all things and remind me of the promises in God's Word. You know what my future holds (John 14:26–29).

Trusting God for Stability

God, I've done everything I can to make things right, and now I am doing what I should have done first—I'm letting go! Do what You will with everything I've held so tightly to. I don't need to be in control. I give it all to You now. Help me to leave it with You and not pick it back up. I'll do only what You ask me to do—nothing more.

I will say of the LORD, "He is my refuge and
my fortress, my God, in whom I trust."
PSALM 91:2

Peaceful Sleep

Lord, You have promised me peaceful sleep. Help me calm my mind and settle my heart. I push my thoughts and concerns for tomorrow out of my head. I put my mind on Your goodness, mercy, and love. I remind myself of the many things I am thankful for. As I sleep, I know You are with me. My body and soul rest safely, knowing that You watch over me all night long. Help me to wake up energized and ready for another day with You.

Facing the Unexpected

Lord, I'm outside my comfort zone. I am dealing with so many things for the first time. I don't know what to expect. I am afraid of what is about to happen. Comfort me and help me to focus on You. Help me to guard my words and respond with Your love, no matter how fearful I am of the outcome.

No need to panic over alarms or surprises, or predictions that doomsday's just around the corner, because GOD will be right there with you; he'll keep you safe and sound.
PROVERBS 3:25–26 MSG

Breaking Fear's Grip

God, I admit that sometimes fear grips me. I want to be strong in faith, but sometimes circumstances are just too much. Help me to recognize fear and draw strength from You, so I can break fear's grip when it begins to overwhelm me. Forgive me when I try to handle life on my own. I want to depend on You, but sometimes it's hard to let go. Teach me how to trust You, since I know You are more than able to deal with any circumstance I encounter.

Trusting God for My Future

My life is an obstacle course filled with things that try to keep me off balance. But I draw strength from You. When I pray, I know You hear me. You make plans for me to have a successful life and a prosperous future. I cannot fail because You are directing me as I look to You for guidance. Thank You, Lord, that no matter how many times I fall, You always reach down to take my hand and help me up again.

If God is for us, who can be against us?
ROMANS 8:31

The Promise of Eternal Life

Lord, please remind me that death cannot hold me, just as it could not hold You on Your resurrection day. Help me to stay focused on You and what I can do for You and others that will make an eternal difference. I refuse to allow the fear of death to keep me from living in the here and now. Once I've fulfilled the destiny You have for me, then I will spend eternity with You. Help me to imagine my beautiful future with You while I live a life transformed today by Your power.

Hope for the Battle

Father, I am tired and afraid. My circumstances seem hopeless, and I just want to quit. Your Word tells me to be strong and courageous. I am young and just starting out. I know it won't always be this difficult. Fill me with Your power and provide me with a way of escape. Hold me up and don't let me fall. Give me fresh hope for the days ahead.

"For the LORD your God is the one who goes with you,
to fight for you against your enemies, to save you."
DEUTERONOMY 20:4 NASB

Trusting God for Success

Sometimes I am too afraid to try because I fear I will fail. But Your Word says the same spirit and power that raised Christ from the dead lives in me. Lord, help me to hear from You regarding the things I am to do. I am listening to Your wisdom and I know that even when I come up short, I am still a success because I am becoming who You created me to be.

Shut the Door to Fear

Heavenly Father, help me to recognize the presence of fear, and give me the courage to resist it by faith. I am Your child; I belong to You. Fear has no place in my life. Just as King David encouraged himself in the Lord, I encourage myself by remembering the great things You have done for me. I choose to keep fear out of my life like a homeowner keeps an intruder from breaking into his home.

For God has not given us a spirit of fear,
but of power and of love and of a sound mind.
2 TIMOTHY 1:7 NKJV

Feeling Alone

Sometimes I feel alone and that nobody understands me. Even in the midst of people, I need Your comfort. Help me to realize You are always with me.

I am convinced that nothing can ever separate us from God's love. Neither death nor life, neither angels nor demons, neither our fears for today nor our worries about tomorrow—not even the powers of hell can separate us from God's love. No power in the sky above or in the earth below—indeed, nothing in all creation will ever be able to separate us from the love of God.
ROMANS 8:38–39 NLT

My Attitude

The Power of My Thoughts

Positive thoughts are one key to a great attitude. Beating yourself up with thoughts that you'll never be good enough, that you don't deserve to be loved, and that you aren't smart enough will ultimately steal your dream—not to mention take the joy out of your life. It's hard to maintain a great attitude when your thinking is negative. But when you believe what God says about you and your circumstances, then you build something beautiful in your heart and mind.

Don't think that positive thinking is enough—it takes faith to rely on God to bring change to your heart and mind. Past experiences have shaped your attitudes and values about the world around you. The apostle Paul challenges us to "not be conformed to this world, but be transformed by the renewing of your mind, that you may prove what is that good and acceptable and perfect will of God" (Romans 12:2 NKJV).

Somewhere along the life-road you've walked, someone has done something to hurt you. Maybe it wasn't even intentional, but you wanted to see this person punished for what they did. You most likely wanted to lash out or pay them back. But God's Word clearly tells you to forgive that person. Depending on how hurt you were, you probably needed some time to sort it all out. Your attitude about that person probably stunk for a while.

God's desire is for you to forgive that person—allow that to sink in and change your thoughts, and eventually you can choose to truly forgive them through your trust in God. It could mean thinking more about God's love and your desire to do His will, rather than thinking about what that person did to you.

The Bible is clear in what we should be thinking about. "Finally, brethren, whatever things are true, whatever things are noble, whatever things are just, whatever things are pure, whatever things are lovely, whatever things are of good report, if there is any virtue and if there is anything praiseworthy— meditate on these things" (Philippians 4:8 NKJV). The truth may be that the person hurt you, but thinking about that situation isn't lovely or a good report.

When you're tempted to think thoughts that contradict who you are in Christ, counteract them with thoughts about how important you are to God. Take the time to pray and ask God to encourage you. Spending time with Him and thinking about how much He loves you can turn your attitude around. Recount to the Lord all the wonderful things He's done for you. Picture yourself doing the things God put you on the earth to do. Choose your thoughts—change your life!

For a More Positive Attitude

Lord, You look into my heart and see the truth of how I think and feel. I won't pretend anymore, because I know I can be real with You. Help me to let go of the things that have hurt and angered me. I don't want those things to be my focus. I want to be focused on You and what You have planned for my life today. Help me to do what I need to do without grumbling, complaining, or pointing fingers at others. Fill me with Your joy and strengthen me with Your love.

Gaining Control of My Thoughts

Sometimes I feel like my thoughts are carrying on a conversation and I'm just observing. I feel out of control. But then I remember that You know me better than I know myself. I remember I have control over my thoughts. I turn them toward You and concentrate on what Your Word says about me. I have the mind of Christ. He lived His life saying and doing what You told Him to say and do—and I can, too.

*"For the LORD searches all hearts and
understands all the intent of the thoughts."*
1 CHRONICLES 28:9 NKJV

Transforming My Thoughts

Father, Your Word says I can choose what to think about. Help me to refuse thoughts that keep me prisoner to things in my past or to worries about my future. My hope is in You. You are my strength and my shield. Transform my thoughts with the truth of Your Word. When I read the Bible, help me to remember Your Word. Then when my mind wanders to matters that bring me down, I will recall what You have to say about them.

Cultivating a Good Attitude

Lord, the Bible tells me life and death are in the power of the tongue. What comes out of my mouth is first planted in my mind as thoughts. Sometimes I say words I don't mean or later regret. Fill my spirit with Your goodness. Your words are healthy to me. Help me to control what I say by thinking about what pleases You before I open my mouth.

May the words of my mouth and the meditation of my heart be pleasing to you, O LORD, my rock and my redeemer.
PSALM 19:14 NLT

Guarding My Mind

Thank You for the helmet of salvation to protect my mind. As I spend time with You and in Your Word, I know I will become more like You. I will guard my mind and refuse to allow negative thoughts to have power over me. Your Word is my weapon to fight the thoughts that oppose who I am in Christ. I will be careful about the things I see and hear because I know they can open my mind to positive or negative thinking. Help me to focus on truth.

Giving Something Completely to God

When I pray, I give my concerns to You, but later I find that I've made them my responsibility again. Somewhere in my thinking I stop trusting You and try to work problems out on my own. I don't need to know how You are going to resolve them. Forgive me for making problems bigger than You, and show me how to give them completely to You.

People with their minds set on you, you keep completely whole, steady on their feet, because they keep at it and don't quit.
ISAIAH 26:3 MSG

An Attitude of Thankfulness

God, I appreciate the good things You put in my life. I know I take them for granted sometimes, and I don't mean to be that way. I get caught up with the fast-paced busyness of all the things I have to do. I need to remember the simple things that bring me joy: a moment of laughter, a smile from a stranger, and those moments when things are actually going right. I appreciate Your kindness and the fact that You made me Your child. Thank You!

To Be More Considerate

I could be more considerate. I admit it—I'm usually thinking of myself instead of someone else. Help me to be more considerate of others. Help me to listen when someone is speaking to me. Show me what You want me to say when someone gives me the opportunity to speak to them.

This you know, my beloved brethren. But everyone must be quick to hear, slow to speak and slow to anger.
JAMES 1:19 NASB

Turning Obstacles into Opportunities

Lord, You know I can get upset when things don't go my way. I think a situation should play out a certain way and, when it doesn't, I lose focus and let it ruin my whole day. Help me to see obstacles as opportunities to maintain my composure. I want to learn to rise above circumstances. Remind me that in the light of eternity a few moments of inconvenience are not worth the effort and energy I waste in negative emotional responses. Give me wisdom to see life from Your perspective— sometimes my way isn't the best way.

An Attitude of Humility

Lord, without You I am nothing. Sometimes I want to rely on myself and do things my own way, but I can't depend on my own morality and virtue. I need Your mercy and grace to become all You created me to be. Help me to be content to be myself. Remind me that I am as good as anyone else, but not better than anyone else. You love equally—You love us all very much!

A Teachable Attitude

Holy Spirit, I invite You to be my teacher, to lead and guide me in all truth. Show me how to let go of selfish desires and listen to Your direction. I'll go where You want me to go today. Help me to focus my energy on Your instruction.

My son, pay attention to what I say; listen closely to my words.
Do not let them out of your sight, keep them within your heart;
for they are life to those who find them and
health to a man's whole body.
PROVERBS 4:20–22

A Desire for Goodness

God, You are good, and I want to be good. You are like a steadfast rock. Everything You do is perfect. You are always fair. You are my faithful God who does no wrong, who is right and fair. Let Your goodness drive my life. Help me to recognize sin and call it what it is—*sin*. No more excuses. I refuse to justify wrongdoing just because it's what I want. If it's wrong, it's not from You and I don't want it in my life. Give me a burning desire to hold on tightly to Your righteousness. In all I do, I want to please You.

An Attitude of Mercy

Lord, when others treat me unfairly, judge me, or take something I feel I deserved, I want to get even. I want to fight for what is mine, but then I feel You urging me to show mercy. It's hard for me to do that.

For the weapons of our warfare are not carnal but mighty in God for pulling down strongholds, casting down arguments and every high thing that exalts itself against the knowledge of God, bringing every thought into captivity to the obedience of Christ.
2 CORINTHIANS 10:4–5 NKJV

An Attitude of Repentance

When I sin, I'm miserable. The weight of my sin puts pressure on my soul. It grips me and makes me feel that I deserve punishment—and I do! But You are always forgiving. Never let me take Your mercy lightly. I'm ashamed, and I don't want to come to You. Give me the courage to tell You the truth about all I've done. Help me always run *to* You—not away from You—when I fail. Then assure me of Your forgiveness and help me to forgive myself. Thank You for loving me, no matter what!

The Power of Financial Wisdom

Dustin sat with his graduating class in a long row of chairs facing the stage as a board member opened the graduation ceremony. Dustin's thoughts weren't on what the speaker was saying. He was watching his father and grandfather sitting in the stands behind the platform. They were father and son, but their paths in life had been very different.

His grandfather had enjoyed a long and simple life. Dustin had spent many hours after school and many summers following his grandfather around his small seven-acre farm. He remembered the days he chased the pickup truck up the driveway as his grandfather returned home from his long day as a heavy-equipment operator. Grandpa always made sure he had a snack left in his lunch box for Dustin. After snacks and while Grandma fixed dinner, Dustin and Grandpa made the rounds to milk the cow, feed the chickens, collect the eggs, and check on ripened tomatoes or watermelons from the garden. Grandpa retired at sixty-five and seemed to enjoy life.

Dustin's eyes rested on his father. He had never spent time at home, constantly climbing the corporate ladder. His wife had left him years ago because she said he loved his job more than he loved her. He had been busy, stressed out, and gruff most of Dustin's childhood. Money was his motivation. After his weekend with Dustin, his father always said, "Gotta make a livin'," when he dropped Dustin off at his ex-wife's house. The visits became more infrequent. The more money he made, the more he felt he needed, and that had meant less time for Dustin.

I hope I am wise like Grandpa when it comes to life choices, Dustin thought. *He made money serve him; instead of spending his life serving money.*

The Bible talks about money and financial resources more than any other earthly topic. King Solomon, for example, was one of the wealthiest and wisest kings to ever live. His words in Proverbs provide practical advice even for today.

Solomon's wisdom wasn't something he was born with, but a gift from God. And God has made His wisdom available to you, as well. If you want to make wise decisions in your finances and all the other areas of your life, all you have to do is ask. James 1:5 promises, "If any of you lacks wisdom, he should ask God, who gives generously to all without finding fault, and it will be given to him."

Look to God as your source—He gives you everything you need. He knows what you need before you ask Him—but He still wants you to ask. Ask Him to help you make wise financial decisions and to keep finances in the right perspective.

Guidance in My Finances

God, I ask for wisdom and guidance as I manage my finances. Help me to plan ahead and set realistic goals. Teach me the difference between needs and wants—write it plainly upon my heart and mind. And then show me how to spend my time and money appropriately. As I grow in financial resources, direct me in knowing where the income should go.

> *When his master saw that the LORD was with him*
> *and that the LORD gave him success in everything*
> *he did, Joseph found favor in his eyes.*
> GENESIS 39:3–4

Content Whatever the Circumstances

Father, I am learning to be content whatever the circumstances. I know what it means to be in need, and I know what it is like to have plenty. I have learned the secret of being content in any and every situation, whether well-fed or hungry, whether living in plenty or in want. But You said I could call on You and tell You my troubles. So here I am. You know what I want and what I need. I trust that You will meet all my needs according to Your rich mercy and love in Christ Jesus.

The Power of Credit

Credit is sucking the life out of me. It sounded good to establish credit with a credit card. I just got a little behind at first, and now I'm in way over my head. I am sorry that I purchased more than I could afford. Show me how to pay my creditors quickly. Remind me to consider all options prayerfully before taking on debt.

> *Owe nothing to anyone — except for your obligation to love one another. If you love your neighbor, you will fulfill the requirements of God's law.*
> ROMANS 13:8 NLT

Open the Windows of Heaven

When things are difficult financially, Lord, help me to remain generous. God, help me never to make decisions motivated by fear and financial insecurity. As I give a tenth of my income to You, You have promised to open up the windows of heaven and pour out a blessing that I can't contain. You are always faithful to provide for me. Let my motives be pure—I don't give to get, but my giving produces a blessing. Remind me that the only way to gain true financial security is by trusting in You.

Every Gift Is from God

Everything I have comes from You. Remind me that I am only a custodian of Your gifts. I want to honor You, Lord, with my wealth. Help me to put You first in everything I do. Never let me be deceived into believing that wealth provides me with happiness.

I know what it is to be in need, and I know what it is to have plenty.
I have learned the secret of being content in any and every situation,
whether well fed or hungry, whether living in plenty or in want.
PHILIPPIANS 4:12

Learning to Save Money

It's so hard to watch money sit in the bank. It doesn't seem to be growing fast, but it's important to save for my future. Help me when I'm tempted to buy something impulsively. I want to make good decisions and purchase things that will add value to my life and my relationship with You. Tap me on the shoulder and remind me that I'm not just saving money, but I'm investing in my future. And when it comes time to invest in a major purchase, give me peace in my decision—let me know I'm doing the right thing.

For Honesty in Money Matters

Lord, help me to remain honest in everything I do. I want to be known as a person of integrity. Show me how to do what is just and right. I want to be fair to those I work for and work with. I never want to be perceived as someone who takes advantage of others for my own personal gain.

*Use only one weight, a true and honest weight, and one measure,
a true and honest measure, so that you will live a long time
on the land that GOD, your God, is giving you.*
DEUTERONOMY 25:15 MSG

To Be Debt-Free

Your Word says, "Just as the rich rule the poor, so the borrower is servant to the lender" (Proverbs 22:7 NLT). I want to be debt-free. Help me to remember that cash is the best option. Give me patience to save up for the things I want and need. Remind me that more is not always better. Help me to pay my debts as quickly as possible. Provide me with opportunities to make extra money and then help me to be diligent to put that money toward the debt I owe instead of toward something I want.

As unto the Lord

It's easy to get tired and disgruntled at my job. I have high expectations and can easily let others disappoint me. I don't think they see my potential or appreciate me. Remind me to do my job knowing You are my true boss. You provided me with this job so I could have income. Help me to do my best each day and represent You well. Lord, bless everything I put my hand to, that I may prosper and bring honor to You.

Never be lazy, but work hard and serve
the Lord enthusiastically.
ROMANS 12:11 NLT

The Power of Generosity

Lord, remind me that everything I have belongs to You—You made a way for me to have it. It wasn't anything I did in my own power that brought me to where I am today. Your love and provision have taken care of me. Help me to recognize what I can give in return. You have blessed me to be a blessing to others. Help me not to hold on to things but to share freely with others as You direct me. Give me wisdom in where You want me to give.

The Power of Tithing

God, You have asked me to bring my tithe to You. I honor You in my giving as I set aside a tenth of all You have blessed me with. I am thankful for the many opportunities You have made available to me. I am grateful for the kindness You show me and make available from every person I meet. Thank You for Your promise to open the windows of heaven and pour out a blessing that I cannot contain as I give a portion of what You have given me back to You.

A Right Perspective of Money

Lord, help me to look at money as something that serves me as I serve You. I refuse to let the things money can buy be a substitute for my relationship with You. Money will never make me happy or satisfy me. My attention and focus is on You, Lord. Help me never to make a decision based on the pursuit of money, but help my heart forever pursue knowing You.

A good man leaves an inheritance for his children's children,
but a sinner's wealth is stored up for the righteous.
PROVERBS 13:22

Financial Crisis

Father, I need Your help. Give me wisdom and understanding in what I should do in this financial crisis. I don't know where the money will come from to take care of this situation, but You do. Forgive me for the choices I've made that could have caused these circumstances. Help me to listen to You more closely and make better decisions in the future. Show me the best way to deal with all this. Please give me the goodwill of everyone involved so I can resolve this quickly in a way that pleases You.

For Creative Ideas

God, You are the Creator of the Universe. You knew every idea before it was thought by anyone. You understood every invention before it was dreamed up. Please give me creative ideas for ways to generate income. Help me to be innovative in developing these ideas and show me what You would have me do with them.

Careful planning puts you ahead in the long run;
hurry and scurry puts you further behind.
PROVERBS 21:5 MSG

My Ministry

The Power of Being Real

Reality television seems to catch people in the act of everyday life, showing all the world the truth about those involved in sometimes normal—and not so normal—situations. What if you lived your life similar to a reality show, where the world could look in and see the real you, transparent at all times?

Do you ever find yourself pretending to be someone you're not? How many times have you hidden your emotions and told someone you were okay when your feelings were hurt or you were angry? Maybe there were times when you told people what you thought they wanted to hear instead of being truthful with them.

In the book *Unchristian* by David Kinnaman and Gabe Lyons, a major research project conducted by The Barna Group explains that Christianity has an image problem. The study provides detailed insight into the opinions of sixteen- to twenty-nine-year-olds, demonstrating that Christians have almost completely failed in one of their most important assignments—representing Christ to the world.

Today Christians are perceived as being no different than those outside the church. Christians deal with the same problems as unbelievers. The divorce rate; debt and mental, emotional, and physical-appearance issues are no different. Looking from the outside in, it doesn't appear that Christians have anything to give the world.

People are looking for answers. They are disappointed to find that even those who believe in a loving God are indifferent toward pointing others to Him with the same mission and vision that Jesus demonstrated. Jesus was unconventional. He opposed the religious, man-made interpretations of the law and looked to the heart of those who were outcasts, sick, and hurting. He cared about the ones society ignored.

God wants us to set ourselves apart for His service. We are called to be examples to those who do not know Him. We have to get outside the four walls of the church and live in a way that demonstrates to others what God is like. Like Jesus, we must say and do only what the Father tells us to say and do. We must be real—true to the Word of God, following Jesus, and modeling His example. He demonstrated love for the lost, those society had thrown away. He came to testify to the truth that God loves each one of us.

As you graduate and move to the next level of life, ask God to show you the power of living a transparent life. Let Him help you shake off the facade of what you believe others would want you to be and step into the light of God's truth.

Genuine Authenticity

Lord, help me to be a true reflection of Your heart in all that I do. Help me to take off the mask when I'm tempted to hide my true self. Remind me that my actions should not be for attention, praise, or position. I want my motives to always be pure. Help me to discern my real intentions when I decide to do something. Keep me honest and remind me that I represent You in the choices I make. In everything I pursue, help me above all to be committed to my relationship with You.

Real Relationship

God, I want to be real in my relationships. I want others to see You working in my life. Help me to shift my focus from myself to those around me. I don't want my life to be consumed by empty religion and man-made rules. May my words be a reflection of a heart that is full of Your love and Your life.

"These people make a big show of saying the right thing,
but their heart isn't in it."
MATTHEW 15:8 MSG

When Others Oppose Me

Jesus, sometimes I am tempted to believe I am more spiritual and deserving than others. I know You don't condone that attitude. It makes me angry when others make fun of what I believe, and I am ready to defend my beliefs. Help me to consider their feelings and the possibility that they don't understand where I'm coming from. Remind me that being right is less important than being Your servant. Help me to be a positive influence for those You bring into my life.

Legitimate Faith

Lord, I don't want to fake it! I'm tired of saying one thing and doing another. Forgive me for pretending to have it all together. I don't want to be a wishy-washy Christian. Help me to trust You and believe the promises You have given me in Your Word. I believe—help my unbelief.

*So when you give to the needy, do not announce it with trumpets,
as the hypocrites do in the synagogues and on the streets, to be honored
by men. I tell you the truth, they have received their reward in full.*
MATTHEW 6:2

To Live What I Believe

Lord, forgive me when my choices don't line up with what I say I believe. Help me to nurture Your Word in my heart so I grow to maturity. Teach me Your ways and give me understanding of Your instructions. Allow the values of my faith to affect every area of my life. Convict me of sin when I am tempted to stray from truth. Help me to stay committed to living what I believe as I grow in faith and in my relationship with You.

To Stay Connected

God, there are so many distractions—so many things I feel I have to do. Help me to stay connected to You throughout my day. I want to share it with You and be used by You to reach others. Speak to my heart and remind me that You have something for me to do today. Lead me by Your Spirit.

> *Walk by the Spirit, and you will not*
> *carry out the desire of the flesh.*
> GALATIANS 5:16 NASB

Fill Me with Love

God, You are love. Everything You do is because of love. I want to be a catalyst of love in the lives of others, too. Forgive me when I think first of myself. Help me to prefer others. Help my love for others to grow. Give me compassion and opportunities to demonstrate it. Lord, it's not about me; it's about You and those You want to touch through me. Help me learn to let Your love flow through me to others.

For Boldness in Ministry

Lord, I don't know where to start in sharing my faith with others. When You give me the opportunity, help me to realize You are opening the door. Help me to recognize Your timing and to follow Your leading. Speak to me and through me. Give me Your words that will touch others' hearts and turn them toward a relationship with You.

> *I am not ashamed of the gospel, because it is the power of*
> *God for the salvation of everyone who believes:*
> *first for the Jew, then for the Gentile.*
> ROMANS 1:16

Sharing My Challenges

Father, You know all I have gone through in my life, all of my hurts and pains. I know I went through those difficulties for a reason, perhaps to encourage others. Help me to be quick to share with anyone who might benefit from what I have endured. Help me to share how I learned to trust in You as You brought me through each challenge. Strengthen those people with boldness and courage. Give me the words to encourage them to hold tightly to You during their hardships.

When Others Are Watching

It's hard to be an example, Lord. I don't do everything the way I know I should. I want to be strong and diligent to do what is right. Help me hold fast to my convictions. Help me to be honest when I make mistakes. I want to encourage others by following You faithfully. Give me courage and strength to live my life to please You so I can say to them, "Follow me, as I follow Christ."

> *Be an example to the believers with your words,*
> *your actions, your love, your faith, and your pure life.*
> 1 Timothy 4:12 NCV

For a Soft Heart

God, there is so much I don't know. Sometimes I think I know a lot, but then I realize how much I have to learn. Forgive me for doing all the talking. Teach me to listen to You first, and teach me how to listen to others. Show me how to discern what they are really saying and wanting. Remind me that people aren't always looking for me to solve their problems. Sometimes they just need someone who will be there for them and listen. Help me to be that person.

Keeping My Two Cents

Father, You created me with an opinion about everything. I make the mistake of thinking that people value my opinion. Help me to keep my opinions to myself and instead share what You want me to say. Use me, Lord, to speak Your Word and Your wisdom into their lives. Remind me that I am to be about my Father's business. I want to be ready to speak a word at the right time—but only if that Word comes from You.

> *Keep your tongue from speaking evil*
> *and your lips from telling lies!*
> PSALM 34:13 NLT

Finding the Real Me

Lord, I want to be everything You created me to be. Graduation separated me from my circle of friends, those people I can be myself with. Give me courage to express myself no matter who is around. Help me not to fear what other people think or say about me, but help me to trust You to protect me from potential hurt. Help me to find the real me—the unique person You created me to be. And show me how to express myself in ways that honor You.

Inside and Out

God, I want to live from the inside out. I want people to experience the real me every time we meet. Help me to examine the values that direct my life. Help me to know what I believe and why I believe it. You know the things I struggle with. Give me Your grace and strength as I learn and grow in those areas. I want to honor You in everything I do.

Provide people with a glimpse of
good living and of the living God.
PHILIPPIANS 2:15 MSG

My Education

The Power of Knowledge

Just because you've graduated doesn't mean it's time to stop your education. You may be surprised to find that being a willing student outside the classroom is just as important as the time you spent cracking the books in school.

Everything God created was made to grow, and that includes your wisdom and understanding of the things of God. As a Christian, you will forever be a student of His. You even have your own personal instructor, the Holy Spirit. "You have received the Holy Spirit, and he lives within you, so you don't need anyone to teach you what is true. For the Spirit teaches you everything you need to know, and what he teaches is true—it is not a lie. So just as he has taught you, remain in fellowship with Christ" (1 John 2:27 NLT).

The Spirit of God is diligently at work doing a makeover within your heart so you become a reflection of His image, but He needs your cooperation. Reading the Bible fills your mind with what God says and thinks. When you make Bible time a priority, it will cause you to grow in your faith quickly. Through His Word, you are constantly discovering who He is and who He created you to be.

Your prayer life is your lifeline to growing in God. As you spend time talking to Him and listening to His voice speak to your heart, you come to know Him.

Jesus said, "I tell you the truth, the man who does not enter the sheep pen by the gate, but climbs in by some other way, is a thief and a robber. The man who enters by the gate is the shepherd of his sheep. The watchman opens the gate for him, and the sheep listen to his voice. He calls his own sheep by name and leads them out. When he has brought out all his own, he goes on ahead of them, and his sheep follow him because they know his voice. But they will never follow a stranger; in fact, they will run away from him because they do not recognize a stranger's voice" (John 10:1–5).

Just as you know the voices of those who love you—your family, close friends, and others—you come to recognize the voice of God. In the same respect, when a stranger speaks, that voice is unfamiliar to you, just as the stranger's voice was unfamiliar to the sheep. You grow in your relationship with God and learn to respond to His direction as He teaches you the way He wants you to go and what He wants you to do.

The more time you spend with Him, the more aware you are of His presence. As you find out more about Him, you uncover the characteristics within yourself that reflect His likeness. His direction and guidance will help you be successful as you transition to your next step in life.

To Know You, Lord

Heavenly Father, I am Your child. I belong to You. I want to know You more. Give me understanding of who You are and what You are like. Teach me the things that are important to You so they can become important to me. Help me to put You first in my life. Give me wisdom to choose time with You and to eliminate distractions that keep me too busy for You.

> *"I want you to show love, not offer sacrifices. I want you to know me more than I want burnt offerings."*
> HOSEA 6:6 NLT

To Hear His Voice

God, I want to hear Your voice. I want to know You are speaking to my heart about Your will for my life. Just as the sheep follow the shepherd's voice and pay no attention to the stranger's words, help me to shut out strange voices so I may hear You clearly. Give me patience to listen—and not talk. What You have to tell me is much more important than what I have to say. Help me to experience Your presence as I wait on You. Nothing is more important than time with You.

To Understand the Bible

The Bible is Your Word for my life. Help me to understand what You are saying to me through it. Give me wisdom and understanding as I allow scripture to feed my spirit and fill me with Your strength. I read Your words so I can grow and learn more about You. Bring the words I read back to mind when I need to apply them to the circumstances I face.

> *You made me and formed me with your hands.*
> *Give me understanding so I can learn your commands.*
> PSALM 119:73 NCV

Living in the Real World, Now

School used textbooks to prepare me for the world, but now it's time to experience it for myself. Give me wisdom and help me to apply what I've learned in school to my new environment outside the classroom. Prepare me for the things school didn't prepare me for. Be with me in every situation and show me how to deal with each day, making good decisions and right applications for a successful life.

Learn to Talk to Your Boss

Lord, thank You for my job and for giving me the support of my boss. Sometimes it can be intimidating to talk to my supervisor. I hate it when my mouth goes dry and my hands get sweaty. Fill me with Your confidence. Give me words to speak and the courage to say the things that need to be said. I was hired to do a job, and I will do it well because I know You are with me.

> *Trust in the LORD with all your heart;*
> *do not depend on your own understanding.*
> PROVERBS 3:5 NLT

Asking for Help

Lord, You know I hate asking for help, but I need to learn to rely on others. Some things I can't do by myself, and You created me to need other people. Direct me to the ones I should ask for help. Remind me to appreciate their help and not take it for granted. Give me words to express how much their assistance means to me. Help me to be open-minded if the way they want to help is not what I expected.

To Know the Truth

Lord, thank You for making absolute truth available. You came into the world to testify for truth. It is not relative to what I think or feel. Truth is objective and is based on Your Word, the Bible. Help me to know the truth and see it clearly in my life.

*We know also that the Son of God has come and has
given us understanding, so that we may know him who is true.
And we are in him who is true—even in his Son Jesus Christ.
He is the true God and eternal life.*
1 JOHN 5:20

For Mentors

God, You put people in my life to mentor me. Give me discernment so I know who is a gift from You and who is not. Help me to open up to mentors and receive their counsel. Forgive my pride when I think I know the answers. Let me learn from their mistakes as well as their successes. Help me to be a good student. Teach me to apply Your principles to my life and recognize them as I experience the road You have destined me to travel.

Seeking the Right Knowledge

God, You know everything. All I want to know is already known by You. Teach me to seek truth in a way that pleases You. I don't want to use what I *think* I know of You or Your Word to look good in front of other people. Help me to keep my motives pure. I never want to seek knowledge that is separate from You. Help me to know You by listening to You and observing what You do. I don't just want to know Your Word; I want to put it into practice. I want to live it out loud every day.

Discovering Leadership

Heavenly Father, I want to understand how to become a leader. Jesus led by serving others. He gave of Himself freely to show us the way to truth. Teach me what it takes to lead as I begin by following You and the leaders You placed in my life. Give me a heart to serve and the patience to not take shortcuts in the lessons You want me to learn.

> *It is senseless to pay tuition to educate a fool,*
> *since he has no heart for learning.*
> PROVERBS 17:16 NLT

Paying Attention

God, as I am learning and growing in You daily, teach me to be attentive to Your instruction. Do not let me forget what I have learned from You. Remind me of the amazing and miraculous things You have done to bring me to where I am today. Help me to stand firm in my faith, not just knowing what I believe, but living it. Keep me alert and cautious about people or things that would distract and hinder me from growing in You.

A Concentrated Focus

Lord, fatigue is the enemy of my faith. I refuse to grow weary in my walk with You. Help me to make You the center of all my activities. Give me a clear perception of my relationship with You, that I may learn Your ways and understand my place in Your plan. Like a beam of light breaks through the darkness, break through my mental fog, Lord, and teach me how to focus my attention on You.

> *Ezra had devoted himself to the study and observance*
> *of the Law of the LORD, and to teaching its*
> *decrees and laws in Israel.*
> EZRA 7:10

Learning in the Circumstances

God, teach me how to tune out the voice of my circumstances, the busyness of my life, and the noise surrounding me. My situation hasn't changed, but my attitude has. My hope is in You. Help me to focus on Your promises instead of the circumstances that are shouting at me. I open my heart to listen to Your instruction. Teach me to go to the still waters of Your Spirit and find strength. Peace like a river speaks to me.

The Power of Wisdom

Father, I am listening to Your instruction. I will hide Your Word in my heart and I will not forget what You have done for me. I want to experience Your blessings. I will keep Your commandments, not just because You said to, but because I love You. Give me Your wisdom, Lord. Help me to gain understanding.

They won't go to school to learn about me, or buy a book called God in Five Easy Lessons. They'll all get to know me firsthand, the little and the big, the small and the great.
HEBREWS 8:11 MSG

My Passion

The Power of the Heart

Undoubtedly you've felt your heart tremble at all that's going on in your life as a graduate. So many emotions: excitement, enthusiasm, uncertainty, pride. What is the fuel that fires the passion in your heart?

The word *passion* can describe romantic feelings; a drive to excel in sports, business, or a dream; or how someone feels about material items they collect. In the context of Jesus's life, *passion* means to suffer. It is to want something so badly that you're willing to sacrifice anything to have it. God's desire to have a relationship with you was so great that He sacrificed His only Son to have the opportunity to be a part of your life for all eternity.

St. Augustine is accepted by most scholars as the most important figure in the ancient Western church. His prayer, "For you have created us for yourself, O Lord, and our hearts are restless until they rest in thee," demonstrates the passionate cry of the human heart for something bigger than itself.

Unfortunately, people worldwide spend their lives searching for fulfillment from something or someone other than God. In their search, they substitute God's place in their hearts with false passions such as careers, sports, and relationships.

Is getting to know God your passion? Is it so important to you that, just as Jesus did for you, you're willing to make sacrifices to spend time with Him? When you are passionate about His purpose for your life, then you're willing to do whatever it takes to live for Him.

In Romans 15, the apostle Paul is clear—it is his ambition to bring the knowledge of Christ to everyone. Paul's dramatic encounter with Jesus on the road to Damascus changed his life radically. Knowing Jesus and sharing Him with others consumed Paul for the rest of his life.

The Word of God says, "He has also set eternity in the hearts of men; yet they cannot fathom what God has done from beginning to end" (Ecclesiastes 3:11). Often we think of eternity as a future event—our time in heaven—but eternity is *now*. As soon as you received Jesus as your Savior, you became a part of the eternal family of God. What you do today—what you invest your passion in—is a part of your eternal life.

As you discover your passion for the things of God, your desires for success and a meaningful life come full circle. You learn the true meaning of life.

Start living your forever life now, with a heart passionate toward the things of God.

Growing in Passion toward God

God, I am growing in faith as I get to know You better. I know You first by what You have done for me. You have saved me from darkness and transformed me. You have given me purpose and meaning. Thank You for reaching down and changing my life. I want to become passionate about the things that are important to You. Teach me what I need to know to complete the destiny You have given me. Time with You is a delight as I get to know and understand Your will for my life.

Passionate in Prayer

Father, I realize prayer is important for building a strong relationship with You. Jesus prayed constantly and consistently. People in relationships talk to one another. I never want to neglect my relationship with You. Help me to be faithful to You in prayer. I want to be open to hearing Your voice at all times.

A good person produces good things from the treasury of a good heart, and an evil person produces evil things from the treasury of an evil heart. What you say flows from what is in your heart.
LUKE 6:45 NLT

When God Seems Silent

God, forgive me for the times I walked away, too busy or self-absorbed to stay connected to You. I expect You to be upset with me, and I feel guilty, but Your love for me is unconditional. It's hard to trust when You are silent, but help me to do just that. And forgive me for the times when You were speaking and I wasn't listening. Help me to run to You instead of from You, so You can restore me to Yourself.

Developing a Passion for the Bible

Father, help me to make daily Bible study as much a part of my life as eating. Remind me that the Bible is more than a book, that it contains words revealing Your love for me. Holy Spirit, speak to my heart and tell me what I need to discover each day. Bring what I've read back to my memory so I can meditate on what Your Word is saying to me personally.

Draw near to God and He will draw
near to you. Cleanse your hands, you sinners;
and purify your hearts, you double-minded.
JAMES 4:8 NASB

Being Passionate about the Right Things

Forgive me, Lord, when I am tempted to love things that are pretty to look at or make me feel good about myself. I want to stay focused on You. Help me to eliminate anything that competes with knowing You. Remind me when my natural desires are not in line with what You would have me pursue. I want to love what You love and hate what You hate. Help me to get rid of things in my life that keep me from serving You with all that I am.

What Pleases God

God, I want to be passionate about the purpose You have for me. Show me the things in my life that please You and give me the courage and strength to pursue those things. Keep my purpose before me, fill my heart, and give me right motives to accomplish all You have set before me. As long as You are with me and my focus is on what pleases You, I cannot fail.

How much more shall the blood of Christ, who through the eternal Spirit offered Himself without spot to God, cleanse your conscience from dead works to serve the living God?
HEBREWS 9:14 NKJV

When I've Been Hurt

God, teach me to guard my heart above all else, because it determines the course of my life. I want to learn how to keep painful experiences from destroying me. I refuse to replay what happened over and over in my mind. Help me to let go of it. I don't want to think about the people involved, so help me to let them go by forgiving them. I ask You, Holy Spirit, to do a mighty work in my heart right now. Take what the enemy of my soul meant to harm me and turn it for my good.

For a Restored Soul

Lord, in pursuit of what I thought should be my passion, my soul has been wounded. I am here to ask You for encouragement and strength. I'm not a quitter, but I need to make some major heart adjustments. Guide me with Your Word and speak to me through preaching and teaching. Show me how to ask for help, and bring people who love me and Your Word into my life to give me godly counsel.

> *He restores my soul; He leads me in the paths*
> *of righteousness for His name's sake.*
> PSALM 23:3 NKJV

Freedom from Wrong Passions

God, I have sinned against You, and I feel so guilty. Help me to come boldly before Your throne of grace and accept Your forgiveness. Help me to forgive myself. Forgive me for accepting a counterfeit to the truth. Today I am letting go of wrong passions and embracing a stronger desire for You, Lord. I thought I was strong enough to be exposed to something like this—but I wasn't ready. Help me to separate myself immediately from any relationships that jeopardize my commitment to You.

Standing Up for My Faith

Heavenly Father, I want to let my light shine before all people. Teach me to live and act in a way that speaks Your truth to others. Fill me with an undying passion to see lives changed for Your glory. When I'm called to defend my faith, help me to do it in love, with gentleness and respect.

Let the message about Christ, in all its richness, fill your lives. Teach and counsel each other with all the wisdom he gives. Sing psalms and hymns and spiritual songs to God with thankful hearts.
COLOSSIANS 3:16 NLT

The Pursuit of Diligence

Lord, in all I do in pursuit of You, help me to be diligent. Help me to stay on task and accomplish my work faithfully and responsibly. No matter what work is set before me, I want to be motivated to do it as though I am doing it for You and not for others.

When Overcome with Compassion for Others

Lord, I appreciate You giving me sensitivity toward others. It makes me who I am. Yet, honestly, I am worn out from caring for others. There is so much drama in the lives of my friends and family members, and I can't give when I'm exhausted emotionally. Instruct me in Your wisdom about who I should give my time to. Show me when and where to take time for myself. Help me to know when I need to stop giving to others and take care of myself.

Waiting on God

My feet are positioned at the starting line. I'm ready to run the race. All I need now is Your signal for me to begin it. I believe I've found my passion and I'm ready to act on it, but I know I need to wait for Your timing. Help me to be patient. Alert me to what I still need to do in making my preparations.

> *I long, yes, I faint with longing to enter the courts*
> *of the Lord. With my whole being, body and soul,*
> *I will shout joyfully to the living God.*
> Psalm 84:2 nlt

Fuel for My Passion

Lord, I am beginning to discover my passion for the things that concern You. I am ready to embrace Your meaning for my life. You know what I need to fuel my passion. Make it come alive in my heart. There is a fire burning in my soul to do what You have called me to do. Set things in motion to help me achieve the dream You gave me. Help me to hold tight to this passion and never let the fire in my soul burn out.

My Health

The Power to Live a Long Life

God wants you to live a long and healthy life. In Psalm 91:16 (MSG), He said, "I'll give you a long life, give you a long drink of salvation!"

There is a powerful connection between your physical body and your emotional, relational, and spiritual health. Everyone has a path to choose: life or death. In Deuteronomy 30:19 (NLT) God said, "Today I have given you the choice between life and death, between blessings and curses. Now I call on heaven and earth to witness the choice you make. Oh, that you would choose life, so that you and your descendants might live!"

When you think of a healthy person, you probably first consider their physical condition, but the truth is that physical health can depend on one's spiritual health. In a letter to a friend, the apostle John said, "I pray that you may prosper in all things and be in health, just as your soul prospers" (3 John 1:2 NKJV). Here John hints that our spiritual health is tied to other facets of our health.

The true picture of health encompasses the whole person—the real you. You are created in the image of God. Like Him, you are a spirit. That spirit lives in a body, and you also have a soul made up of your mind, will, and emotions. A long life requires balance in every area of your life. You nurture your spirit by feeding it God's Word and spending time in God's presence through prayer and worship. You take care of your body by eating right, exercising, and getting regular health care and the right amount of rest. Your soul requires affirming words and emotional support for strong mental health.

Many people miss God's best when they receive forgiveness for their sins but hold grudges against those who have hurt them. Unforgiveness holds their soul captive. God clearly commands us to let go and always be willing to forgive. "And do not grieve the Holy Spirit of God, with whom you were sealed for the day of redemption. Get rid of all bitterness, rage and anger, brawling and slander, along with every form of malice. Be kind and compassionate to one another, forgiving each other, just as in Christ God forgave you" (Ephesians 4:30–32).

The Bible is full of promises for you as a child of God. A specific promise in Ephesians 6:1–3 (NCV) says, "Children, obey your parents as the Lord wants, because this is the right thing to do. The command says, 'Honor your father and mother.' This is the first command that has a promise with it—'Then everything will be well with you, and you will have a long life on the earth.'"

As you spend time with God, be open and willing to receive instruction for living a long and healthy life in Him.

Promises for Long Life

God, You have given me so many promises in the Bible. Help me to learn and keep them close to my heart. Thank You for watching over me and promising me a long life. You have given me the opportunity and ability to live according to Your Word. Forgive me when I mess up, and help me to choose life each day. Give me strength to do Your will as I choose right living. As I come to know You better, I pray that I will know with more assurance what You would have me do.

Choose Life

Jesus, You offered me life, not just life after death but eternal life that started the day I asked You to live in my heart. Help me to remember that every choice I make is a choice for life or for death, for blessing or cursing. I don't want to live one day less on the earth because of a poor choice I made. Help me to make every decision count.

> *Today I ask heaven and earth to be witnesses. I am offering*
> *you life or death, blessings or curses. Now, choose life!*
> *Then you and your children may live.*
> DEUTERONOMY 30:19 NCV

My Path of Life

Father, I know the path I choose for my life is important to You. You have delivered me out of spiritual darkness and into the light. Help me to establish order and live a balanced life. Help me to keep Your ways in all I do. I choose Jesus' example and will follow in His footsteps. Remind me, Lord, that I don't have to travel alone, but that Jesus is right here with me. Everywhere I go, as I follow Your instruction, I am in the right place at the right time, and You satisfy me with a long life.

Wisdom for Life

God, I need Your wisdom every day. I know I can't depend on my own common sense. Guide me in everything I do. Help me to be quick to hear Your voice and follow Your direction. When I feel lost, let me be quick to cry out for help. When life gets crazy and I don't know what to do, remind me to call for help and respond to Your wisdom.

She [Wisdom] offers you long life in her right hand,
and riches and honor in her left.
PROVERBS 3:16 NLT

Freedom from Bitterness

Jesus, I'm feeling bitter and angry over the hurt I've endured. These emotions are holding me prisoner. I have to let them go but it's hard. I want to see justice for what has been done to me, but instead I ask You to heal my wounded heart and help me let go of the pain. By faith, I release those who offended me. Cleanse me and make me new. It's hard to say this, but I'm trusting You. Fill me with Your love for those who hurt me. Let me see them through Your eyes of love.

Good Judgment

Lord, I am determined to discount my own wisdom and acknowledge You in all I do. Give me a heart that discerns Your ways from my own and those of the world. Help me to be sensible and practical—I don't want to overthink a situation, but I want to respond to Your direction. Help me to see wisdom as the most valuable thing I could attain.

If you live wisely, you will live a long time;
wisdom will add years to your life.
PROVERBS 9:11 NCV

Living Right

Lord, I realize sin subtracts from my life and right living adds to it. It's a no-brainer, but sometimes my thinking is off balance. Make Your path clear to me. Sometimes trivial things detain me from making right choices. Remind me of Your Word so I make decisions according to Your will. Help me to resist distractions that would keep me from spending time with You. My life is in You, Lord. My hope and expectation for a long life is in You.

To Give Your Life Away

God, I've given my life to You. It no longer belongs to me. I choose to serve You all my life, but I have to remember that or else I fall back into owning my life instead of being a caretaker of it. I ask You to be the master of my destiny.

> *"You shall walk in all the way which the LORD your God has commanded you, that you may live and that it may be well with you, and that you may prolong your days in the land which you will possess."*
> DEUTERONOMY 5:33 NASB

A Healthy Soul

God, my thoughts affect my mind, will, and emotions. When I'm spending too much time thinking about negative things, wake me up. Help me to let go of the thoughts that bring me down. Remind me to think of all that is pure and right. I can't change the past, and it doesn't help to worry about the future. Help me to encourage myself by remembering Your promises for my life. Help me to live my very best life and focus on You.

The First Command with a Promise

Lord, You know I've rebelled against my parents. I'm not making excuses, but I felt I had to find my own way. My attitude and heart were wrong. Forgive me for justifying my words and actions. I'm sorry I hurt them. I repent for not respecting them for the position You gave them in my life. Forgive me, and help them to forgive me, too. Show me ways I can honor them now.

> *"Honor your father and mother. Then you will live a long, full life in the land the LORD your God is giving you."*
> EXODUS 20:12 NLT

To Be Disciplined

Lord, help me to be disciplined in every area of my life. A long life requires taking care of myself. Help me to grow spiritually so I can stand firm in my faith. Hold me accountable for spending time with You each day. Teach me what Your Word says about practical things, like what I eat and drink and put into my body. Give me determination to exercise and eat right. Help me to feed my soul with Your goodness. Lead me to positive relationships with people who share my faith.

Overcoming Discouragement

Father, sometimes my heart is overcome with despair. You know the losses I've faced and the stress I deal with. Forgive me for giving in to hopelessness. Thank You for Your Holy Spirit, who is with me. Strengthen me with Your hope and confidence. Help me to build my faith by walking closely with You and reading Your Word. Show me how to use this difficult time to comfort others. Thank You for saving me from darkness and returning me to the light of Your love.

God's Way of Living

Father, help me to always choose what is just and right according to Your truth. Bring Your commands into my thoughts every time I am tempted to go against Your laws. Remind me of my promises to You. When I choose Your ways, I am assured that my life will be completely balanced in the spiritual, physical, emotional, and relational areas of my life.

My child, never forget the things I have taught you.
Store my commands in your heart. If you do this, you will
live many years, and your life will be satisfying.
PROVERBS 3:1–2 NLT

For Healing

God, You created me for a long and satisfying life. You knit me together in my mother's womb and You know every intricate part of my being. You know what I need before I ask, and I'm asking You to return me to good health. You know how my body and mind work, so You know how to heal me. I refuse to let my health be stolen from me. I am determined to fight for it. Direct me to the right doctors, if that's the way I should go. Give me peace to make the right decisions on my journey to recovery.

My Body

The Power of Purity

A little boy, not more than three years old, looked up at his grandpa. "Poppa, do you have Jesus in your heart?" he asked. "Yes," his grandpa replied. The little boy looked at the cigarette in his grandfather's hand and said, "So, are you making Jesus smoke?"

The apostle Paul, in 1 Corinthians 3:16, asks a similar question, "Don't you know that you yourselves are God's temple and that God's Spirit lives in you?" In a world where sex sells every product imaginable, it can be tough to stand for purity and modesty.

Have you ever watched a horror movie and found it stayed with you? You probably knew you shouldn't watch it, but you convinced yourself it wouldn't bother you. Yet once those images were imprinted on your mind, they were difficult to forget.

You—spirit, soul, and body—are what you eat. Your spirit and mind respond to what you put into them just as your body responds to what you put into it. Caffeine might give you energy, or turkey might make you tired. What you see and hear affects you, too. What you think about fills your mind and enters your heart.

That's why the Bible is clear that we are to think about "whatever is true, whatever is noble, whatever is right, whatever is pure, whatever is lovely, whatever is admirable," things that are "excellent or praiseworthy" (Philippians 4:8).

When you expose yourself to things that contradict what you say you believe, it damages your heart. Your old nature—who you were before you knew the Lord—craves those things that are counter to God. And when you feed the old nature, it gains strength; and at the same time, you starve your spirit from the things of God.

God has set some guidelines in His Word that will keep you on the right road for your life. However, you're going to make mistakes. We all do. The key is to run *to* God instead of *away* from Him when you fail. He loves you more than you can ever know—but you have to trust that He will forgive you and give you a second chance. . .and a third. . .and a fourth. His mercy is new every morning.

As you choose to remain faithful to God, that commitment brings freedom from the negative things that can attach themselves to your life. "And so, dear brothers and sisters, I plead with you to give your bodies to God because of all he has done for you. Let them be a living and holy sacrifice—the kind he will find acceptable" (Romans 12:1 NLT). When you start your new life after graduation, remember that Jesus, your roommate, is there to help you stay true to the commitment you've made to share your life with Him.

A Right Perspective

Father, sometimes I wish I looked different, because there are things about my body that I don't like. Remind me that You knew what I looked like long before I was born. I am wonderfully made by Your hand. Help me to be thankful for how You designed me. I want to be a good steward of the body You gave me. Help me to nurture it, respect it, and celebrate it. My body doesn't belong to me—it belongs to You! And what I do with it reflects on You.

Set Apart

Father, I belong to You. My life—spirit, soul, and body—belongs to You. Forgive me when I choose my own way. When I give in to my own selfish desires, I not only hurt myself, I hurt You. Remind me that I'm set apart for You.

What agreement is there between the temple of God and idols?
For we are the temple of the living God. As God has said:
"I will live with them and walk among them, and I will
be their God, and they will be my people."
2 CORINTHIANS 6:16

For My Body

God, You created my body and gave it to me as a gift. Teach me how to keep it healthy. Give me wisdom and strength to make right choices. Teach me what Your Word says about my body and help me to do what is right. Show me how to control my passions and my appetites so I can live a long and healthy life. Protect me from dangerous addictions. I don't want to be dependent on anything or anyone but You. Help me to be fit for Your service, ready at a moment's notice to do what You ask.

To Be Sexually Pure

Lord, forgive me for the sins of my past. Cleanse me and make me pure. Help me to honor You in all my relationships so that, when the time comes to give myself to my spouse, I can do so with integrity of heart. Help me to keep myself for my spouse until the day You unite our hearts as one.

There is a sense in which sexual sins are different from all others.
In sexual sin we violate the sacredness of our own bodies, these
bodies that were made for God-given and God-modeled
love, for "becoming one" with another.
1 CORINTHIANS 6:18 MSG

Freedom from Pornography

God, I am responsible for what I put in front of my eyes. It is my responsibility to protect myself. Forgive me for looking at pornography. I am ashamed and feel guilty, but am compelled by it. I need help. Give me courage to go to someone I trust who will pray for me and help me be accountable. Show me who that person is. Heal my heart and make me clean again. Convict me when I'm tempted, and draw me close to You. I look to You—You are where my help comes from.

Freedom from Sexual Sin

Father, forgive me. I feel like I'm damaged and beyond repair. I've destroyed something precious and I can't take it back. I'm disappointed in myself for believing the lie that sexual sin was okay. Forgive me for justifying it. I was wrong. Heal my heart and give me hope again.

> *God wants you to be holy and to stay away from sexual sins.*
> *He wants each of you to learn to control your own body in*
> *a way that is holy and honorable. Don't use your body for*
> *sexual sin like the people who do not know God.*
> 1 THESSALONIANS 4:3–5 NCV

Freedom from Substance Abuse

God, forgive me for trying to find comfort in drugs or alcohol to escape reality. I justified it because of the pain I was feeling, and I was wrong. I should have come to You instead of looking to other things to solve my problems. Help me to discern the flaws in my heart that need to change so I can overcome this temptation. Open my heart and expose the truth to me so I can change. Remind me that I can run to You with my problems. You have the answers I need for my life.

Finding a Secure Path

Lord, fill me with Your strength and direct my ways so I can successfully press through the temptation of sin. I want to remain obedient to Your leadership. I don't want to take Your mercy and grace for granted. Help me to focus on what is pure and holy in Your sight.

I made a solemn pact with myself
never to undress a girl with my eyes.
JOB 31:1 MSG

When I'm Tempted

Father, You have promised me a way of escape. I am listening and I want a way out. Help me to stand against all that tempts me. Help me always to choose You over temptation.

The temptations in your life are no different from what others experience. And God is faithful. He will not allow the temptation to be more than you can stand. When you are tempted, he will show you a way out so that you can endure.
1 CORINTHIANS 10:13 NLT

For a Pure Heart

God, create in me a pure heart and a right spirit. Show me all my wrongdoings. Give me the strength to resist the lies that distort my thinking when I try to justify sin. Make me new, like the first day I was born into the kingdom of God. As I fill my mind with Your truth from the Bible, help me to renew my mind with right thinking. Show me Your ways and instruct me in all I do. Guide me with Your eye and direct me with Your truth.

When I Go Online

God, sometimes an innocent Internet search produces a temptation. Those sites I shouldn't visit grab my curiosity, and I am tempted to click. Forgive me for going where I shouldn't. Show me what actions I need to take to stay clear of the things that try to come between me and my commitment to You. If it means giving up the computer, then give me the courage to do that. Remind me that sin separates me from You. I don't want anything to come between me and You. I have a choice, and above all, I choose You!

To Yield to God's Standards

Lord, You know me better than I know myself. You know my internal struggles and the things that challenge me deep within my soul. You created me, and You know what I need. I surrender what I want for what You know I need. You have the highest standards, and I want to meet them. I give myself to Your will and hope with great expectation to live my life according to the standards You have set in place.

I urge you, as aliens and strangers in the world,
to abstain from sinful desires, which war against your soul.
1 PETER 2:11

Purity in My Speech

Father, You created me to be pure like You. Please forgive me when I allow the impure language of the world to come out of my mouth. I have polluted my heart by allowing those thoughts to penetrate my mind. Remove that trash from my heart as I fill up on scriptures. I am responsible for the words I speak. Help me to ask others who heard me speak like that to forgive me, as well. A trash-talker is not who I want to be. When I say words like that, I am not a reflection of You.

Holding Tight to God

My life was an emotional roller coaster until I found You. You are my only hope.

> *Keep me safe, O God, I've run for dear life to you. . . .*
> *Without you, nothing makes sense. . . . The wise counsel GOD gives*
> *when I'm awake is confirmed by my sleeping heart. Day and night I'll*
> *stick with GOD; I've got a good thing going and I'm not letting go. . . .*
> *You canceled my ticket to hell—that's not my destination!*
> *Now you've got my feet on the life path. . . . Ever since*
> *you took my hand, I'm on the right way.*
> PSALM 16:1–2, 7–8, 10–11 MSG

The Power of Shared Faith

School gave you an opportunity to participate in all types of groups. Most likely you were a part of a study group—maybe you were part of a sports team, a class lab, or different social clubs across campus. And every group had a common thread that tied you to that group.

When you accepted Jesus as your Lord and Savior, you became a part of a large group called Christians and a member of God's eternal family. Jesus told His friend and disciple, Peter, "And I also say to you that you are Peter, and on this rock I will build My church, and the gates of Hades shall not prevail against it" (Matthew 16:18 NKJV).

Church can mean an actual building where people meet to worship God, but Jesus wasn't talking about a place. He was referring to all the people who share a common truth—a belief in His salvation message. The church is a living, breathing body of believers who share their faith in God and celebrate His love for them. Religion is man-made, with rules that govern a group of people who submit to that organization. But in *relationship*, the heart of man is what God is most concerned about. Church should serve as a home where God's family comes together.

Church is all about the family of God living, learning, and growing together. God the Father enjoys sharing His presence with you corporately and individually. Hebrews 10:25 instructs us: "Let us not give up meeting together, as some are in the habit of doing, but let us encourage one another—and all the more as you see the Day approaching."

There is strength in shared faith. As believers come together, they grow in every area of their lives. You can grow quickly in wisdom and understanding through the exchange of the Word of God and through corporate worship and praise.

An atmosphere charged with faith delivers amazing results. Much as a natural family supports one another and learns to live with and love one another, Christians do the same within the household of faith.

Jesus said, "Again, I tell you that if two of you on earth agree about anything you ask for, it will be done for you by my Father in heaven" (Matthew 18:19). That is some serious power, and when you have a group of people praying and believing God for something specific, miracles happen.

If you don't have a church home, ask God to show you where you should connect with His family. Church is a wonderful opportunity to practice the truth you've found in Christ. You will discover a group of people who love God and will learn to love you. Within your new family you will find people who will pray and encourage you in the Lord. There are opportunities to serve others in many areas as you grow together.

Church Family

Lord, I pray for my church family. Give us strength to put aside our differences so we can serve You together. Help us to understand and care about one another—just as You care about each one of us. Show me who I can learn from and who should be learning from me. Place me where You want me to be within Your family.

> *You will know how to live in the family of God.*
> *That family is the church of the living God,*
> *the support and foundation of the truth.*
> 1 TIMOTHY 3:15 NCV

Finding a Church

God, I need a church home. I want to share my faith and learn Your wisdom by spending time with other believers. Guide me to a church where Your truth and love are practiced, not just preached. Help me to be bold and to be first to reach out to people You want me to get to know. Thank You for providing me with friendships that will help my faith to grow and give me an opportunity to gain and receive support for the challenges I face. Give me discernment so I know where I belong within Your family.

For My Pastor

God, thank You for giving me a spiritual leader who loves me and You. Help him to always speak Your truth and never stray from it. Surround him with wise counsel, and give him a heart that listens to counsel that ultimately comes from You. Keep him close to You, filled with Your compassion for the people You have placed in our church. Protect him from criticism. Help him to be watchful over our church family, discerning what is Your best. Bless him and his family in everything they do.

To Be a Support to Others

Lord, help me to encourage others every day. Help me to share what I have with others and encourage them. You are my strength, so I will lean on You as others lean on me. Help me to build their faith instead of tearing it down. Help me to be positive and uplifting when people share their troubles with me. When people leave my presence, I want them to feel better than when they came to see me.

> *Let each of you look out not only for his own interests,*
> *but also for the interests of others.*
> PHILIPPIANS 2:4 NKJV

To Go beyond the Four Walls

Jesus, I need Your help. We have become comfortable inside our church. Where is the desire to tell others about You? Teach us how to go outside the four walls of our church building. Speak to the hearts of the people within our church family. Share Your vision to reach out into the community through them. Give us the desire to demonstrate Your love to those who are hurting. Grow in us an eagerness to reach and transform lives through the love of God within us.

More Prayer

Father, You said Your house would be a house of prayer. I ask You to put a burning desire in the hearts of Your people to pray and seek You. Help us to be diligent to pray for You to heal our land, as You promised to do if we prayed. It's great to see people at church, but our purpose is not a social function. We get together to focus on You. Teach us to pray for the things that concern You.

*"For where two or three come together
in my name, there am I with them."*
MATTHEW 18:20

Just Listen

God, Your family is loud. We talk, talk, talk. I'm guilty, too, of thinking I have important things to say. Please forgive me. Even in church, so many of us come with an agenda—before, during, and after church. You are the One with all the answers, and we should be paying attention. Teach us to listen to Your voice, to hear You. Teach us to listen when the world is loud and when we find those quiet moments with You. Help us to discipline ourselves to hear You and to be quick to obey.

When I'm Too Tired

Church can be demanding, especially when I'm serving You in different ministries. Life is busy and I'm tired. Forgive me when I want to stay in bed and shut out the world. Remind me that I need the support and encouragement of others, from the spoken Word at the pulpit to the shouts of joy during praise and worship.

And let us not neglect our meeting together, as some people do,
but encourage one other, especially now that
the day of his return is drawing near.
HEBREWS 10:25 NLT

When I've Been Hurt by the Church

God, Christians should look and act like You, but sometimes they don't. Sometimes I don't.

People shouldn't hurt each other. I want to blame You for their behavior but I can't. I know they were responsible, not You. It makes me want to quit church, but I know that's not what You want. Help them to see what they have done, and keep them from ever doing that to anyone else. Heal my hurts and help me to forgive them. Lead me to people who will build me up in my faith, and help me trust the church again.

Church Vision

Father, thank You for leaders who know where they are going and where they are taking people. Give us everything we need to accomplish the vision You have given us. Give us the people and the finances to do the work. Show us Your perfect timing for each portion of the plan. Bless every person who is serving, as we work together to accomplish Your goal. Help us to be sensitive to others coming into the church who may not understand what we are doing and why. Help us to share the vision with them.

For a Group

Lord, bring me to a group of people devoted to You and Your Word. Knit our hearts together stronger than an earthly family's. Show us how to share our faith with one another in a way that propels us to spiritual growth. Let us be an unbreakable strength for one another when facing things that challenge our faith daily. No matter what we face, help us to depend on You and on each other to carry us through.

[The early church] devoted themselves to the apostles' teaching and to the fellowship, to the breaking of bread and to prayer.
ACTS 2:42

Everyone in Their Place

Lord, we are moving forward as Your family. I ask You to bring new people into our church to help us achieve all You want us to do. Give us a burning desire to fulfill the dream You placed in our hearts. Give people wisdom as to where they belong within our church, where the gifts You have given them can best be used.

Speak encouraging words to one another. Build up hope so you'll all be together in this, no one left out, no one left behind.
1 THESSALONIANS 5:11 MSG

For the Lost

Jesus, You came to earth to save all who were lost. Help us to stop expecting them to come to us. Show us the best way to reach the lost with Your love. Help us to live in a way that points people to You. Remind us that relationship is the key to life transformation. Give us discernment about how we are to lead the lost to You. Help us to see them from Your perspective and remind us that we were once lost, too.

The Power of Church

Thank You for entwining my heart with the hearts of my brothers and sisters in Christ. Teach me to love them, forgive them, know them, and bless them each day. Teach me to pray for them as You lead and guide me in my prayer time. And thank You that I have family I can call on when I need their support, and that we can come to You together for whatever we need.

"If two of you agree here on earth concerning anything you ask,
my Father in heaven will do it for you."
MATTHEW 18:19 NLT

The Power of Worship

Friends and family celebrate you as a graduate by sending you cards and gifts and attending your graduation ceremony and party. They share encouraging words to motivate and inspire you. While that isn't worship, it is a form of praise and admiration for you and what you've accomplished. It gives you a taste of what God might feel when you honor Him for His position in your life and the things He's done for you.

Music has power. It floods your mind with memories you associate with certain songs. It can make you want to smile, dance, cry, or sing along. You might find it difficult to verbalize its strength, but somehow it has the ability to touch the secret places of your soul.

Amazing things happen when people worship God, and music is significant in worship. Music has the power to take us into the throne room of God, into the presence of all of heaven.

There are stories in the Bible where songs of worship brought actual, physical change to a believer's situation. God promised the city of Jericho to the Israelites. In Joshua 6 you read how the blast of trumpets and shouts of praise brought down the city walls. In Acts 16 a violent earthquake shook the prison holding Paul and Silas captive, setting them free, after they'd spent hours singing praise to God.

On Sunday morning, April 29, 1984, a tornado ripped through the small Oklahoma town of Mannford. It leveled the elementary school to its foundation, destroyed most of the high school, and ripped the roofs completely off homes and the local churches near the two schools. Tragically, the F-5 tornado killed one person and left the town in shambles.

People were gathered in their churches just moments before for morning worship, unaware of the storm brewing. Imagine the loss if the tornado had touched down on a weekday. Children from kindergarten through high school could have died. It's possible that worship stopped Satan from using the storm to destroy a town and shatter the lives of everyone in it.

Think about your music. Does it bring you closer to God? Worship invites God into your life. As you praise Him with your time and attention, you give Him a place of honor in your life. When you pray, take time to thank Him for the promises He's made to you in His Word, and you can expect Him to intervene in your circumstances.

To Be an Instrument of Praise

God, You created me to be an instrument of praise. From head to toe, I'll bless Your holy name! I don't want to forget a single blessing. You forgave my sins, healed my diseases, and saved me from hell. You poured out oceans of love and mercy. You wrap me in Your goodness. As high as heaven is over earth, so strong is Your love for me. You know me inside and out—and love me anyway! (from Psalm 103 MSG)

Always remind me how great You are and the wonderful things You have done for me. I shout aloud that You are my God!

Reasons to Celebrate

I am so happy because You are my God! I am bought with a great price, and I thank You for loving me with an everlasting love. You have put a song in my heart, where before I could not sing. In Your presence there is fullness of joy. I will bless You at all times: May Your praises forever be on my lips and a song of joy be in my heart.

Speak to one another with psalms, hymns and spiritual songs.
Sing and make music in your heart to the Lord.
EPHESIANS 5:19

David's Song on the Run

I've run to you for dear life. I'm hiding out under your wings
until the hurricane blows over. I call out to High God, the God who
holds me together. He sends orders from heaven and saves me. . . .
He makes good on his word. . . . I'm ready, God, so ready, ready from
head to toe, ready to sing, ready to raise a tune: "Wake up, soul!". . . .
I'm thanking you, GOD, out loud in the streets, singing your praises
in town and country. The deeper your love, the higher it goes; every
cloud is a flag to your faithfulness. Soar high in the skies, O God!
Cover the whole earth with your glory!
PSALM 57:1–3, 7, 9–11 MSG

In Spirit and in Truth

Father, teach me the true art of worship. I totally surrender
my life to You. Let my life be lived in honor of all that You are.
Let my life shine before all men so they see Your glory. I shout
Your praises wherever I go. Put a continual song of praise in
my heart!

"But an hour is coming, and now is, when the true worshipers will
worship the Father in spirit and truth; for such people the Father
seeks to be His worshipers. God is spirit, and those who
worship Him must worship in spirit and truth."
JOHN 4:23–24 NASB

The Name above All Names

My soul boasts in the Lord. Let the oppressed hear and rejoice. Lord, I called to You and You answered me; You delivered me from all my fears. Your eyes are on me because You have made me righteous in Your sight. As I travel through each trouble, You deliver me out of them all—always providing a way of escape. You redeem me; no one is condemned who takes refuge in You. (Taken from Psalm 34.)

Let us continually offer the sacrifice of praise to God,
that is, the fruit of our lips, giving thanks to His name.
HEBREWS 13:15 NKJV

Freedom from Sin's Punishment

Oh, God!" I shout aloud and rejoice with all my heart. You have taken away my punishment and turned back my enemy. You are with me; never again will I fear any harm. You are mighty to save me. Thank You for calming me with Your love. You dance over me with singing. You have given me praise and honor in every place that I was put to shame. You have freed me from sin's punishment and given me a new life. I have found my hope again. You are an awesome God!

Praise to the God of My Salvation

God of my salvation, You are my everything. You deserve the highest praise. Nothing and no one deserves more adoration from my lips than You. In everything I do I desire to give You the highest admiration. There is nothing too big for You. Every challenge You meet; every adversity You overcome. You are mighty on my behalf because You have made me righteous. You have given me a clean slate through my salvation. You have wiped away the mess and presented me new and ready to be used by You. I am thankful to be called one of Your own.

I Am Blessed

Thank You, God, that You made me Your child. You have given me an inheritance of peace and called me blessed. I am blessed at all times—when I come home and when I go out. Wherever I go, I am rich in favor because I am called by Your name.

"My soul glorifies the Lord and my spirit rejoices in God my Savior,
for he has been mindful of the humble state of his servant. From
now on all generations will call me blessed, for the Mighty One
has done great things for me—holy is his name."
LUKE 1:46–49

Bless the Lord of All

Lord, You established Your throne in heaven, and You rule over all. Creation praises You. You speak and the earth responds. Deep within my spirit, I sing praises to Your name. I honor You with singing and clap my hands. You are miraculous, surprising me with the dreams that You have for me. I will never forget all You have done for me. Thank You for considering me the apple of Your eye. You satisfy my soul with good things. You will never accuse me, but are always gracious. You stir my heart with expectation because You are Lord of all!

Embracing God's Best

From morning to evening, let my life be praise to You. Everything that I say and do I want to bring honor to You. No matter who I am with or what I'm doing, let there be adoration in my heart.

So here's what I want you to do, God helping you: Take your everyday, ordinary life—your sleeping, eating, going-to-work, and walking-around life—and place it before God as an offering. Embracing what God does for you is the best thing you can do for him.
ROMANS 12:1 MSG

Song of Righteousness

Sometimes I don't feel like praising You, but I need to do it by faith. Help me to join the earth in praising You. When I don't have a praise song, help me to find one on the radio or on a CD. Stir up Your gifts within me. Speak to my spirit and awaken it. Give me a new song to sing. When there are no words, help me to make music in my heart that expresses just how much I love You. You are always good to me, Lord. You are the reason I sing.

Rivers of Living Water

God, You are *good!* I love Your Word and want to think about it day and night. You have planted me like a tree near a river. You are continually restoring me so everything I do produces a good result. Thank You for planting me firmly and supplying me with everything I need to grow in You.

So all of us who have had that veil removed can see and reflect the glory of the Lord. And the Lord—who is the Spirit—makes us more and more like him as we are changed into his glorious image.
2 CORINTHIANS 3:18 NLT

Thanksgiving Because You Made Me

Lord, I worship You with gladness. I lift my heart, my voice, and my hands in thankfulness to You. You are the Lord, my God! You—no one else—made me. I am one of Your people. I will come before You with thanksgiving and will praise Your name. You are good, and Your love continues forever, without end. Help me to remember that I am the way I am because You made me this way. And everything You make is good! Thank You for making me who I am and helping me to become all You created me to be.

Jesus, My Forever

Jesus, You are my forever! No matter who comes and goes in my life, You are with me forever. I can depend on You. I know that no matter what mistakes I make, You won't leave me. You stand strong with me in everything I face. You are amazing. You gave Your life so I could spend eternity—starting now— with You. You gave me the greatest gift, and I never want to forget the sacrifice You made for me. You're the *best!*

Worship the LORD with gladness;
come before him with joyful songs.
PSALM 100:2

The Power of Forgiveness

Ah, the past. . .your story of how you arrived at the here and now. When you first meet new people, they often ask who you are and where you come from. Sure, there's no hesitation in telling your accomplishments and what you've achieved to get where you are. Yet you probably aren't as quick to recall the flip side: your embarrassing moments, mistakes, and failures.

Everyone has a past and no one, no matter how perfect they seem to be, is without fault. We come into the world fallen and sinful, thanks to the actions of the first parents—Adam and Eve.

We start out far from God, but when we find Him, we discover He's made a way for us to begin again. Our lives are transformed through salvation. Our past is erased. We are brand new in Him.

Let's say your life was a book. Everything you ever did or said was recorded in it. And the day you went to Jesus and asked Him to forgive you and make you new, He took that old book filled with your secrets, your sins, and your past and tossed it in a shredder. He didn't stop there. He then took the shredded pieces of your story and dumped it into a sea of forgiveness. The waves carried them far from shore, where they sank to the bottom of the sea and dissolved into nothingness.

Then He turned to you and opened a new book, a new

life story with your name on it. The pages are crisp and clean. He offered you a new beginning, a fresh start. Your past is forgotten. In your new book of life your humiliation, guilt, and regret are gone.

This is what it's like every time you go to Him and confess a sin.

You may have trouble forgetting your mistakes, and you may even have trouble forgiving yourself. But as far as God is concerned, you're brand new. You don't have a history. Your mistakes no longer exist and are no longer written in the book. He doesn't remember your sin.

The devil does. He wants to remind you about it so you keep looking back. When you're focused on what *was,* you can't pay attention to what God's set in front of you.

There's a perception that there are little sins and big sins and that it's harder to be forgiven for a big sin. Yet, sin is sin. No matter how big or how small, it separates us from God. It makes us want to run from Him instead of to Him, and the enemy of your soul, the devil, knows that. That's why he wants to make a big deal of your sin.

You have a new story today. Embrace the power of forgiveness. Let go of the pain of the past and press forward to your new life in Christ Jesus. It's the reason Jesus came to Earth—to offer you freedom and peace through your relationship with God. Move forward and don't look back.

When I'm Feeling Guilty

Father, You gave me a fresh start when I received Your gift of salvation, but memories of my past sins find their way to the front of my mind. Remind me that You have wiped the slate clean. My past no longer exists for You. Relieve me of this pressure of guilt—my sin is gone! I let go of it today and refuse to let old memories enslave me. I give them all to You. Help me to create new memories of Your goodness and love for me. Thank You for setting me free.

> *"I will be merciful to their unrighteousness, and their sins and their lawless deeds I will remember no more."*
> HEBREWS 8:12 NKJV

Moving past My Mistakes

God, You don't speak to me according to my past mistakes, and my heavenly rewards are not based on how many times I failed or succeeded. Although I can't erase my past, You can—and have. Thank You for removing my transgressions and filling me with Your great love and kindness in exchange. Help me to learn from my past and to move forward.

"The thief comes only to steal and kill and destroy;
I have come that they may have life, and have it to the full."
JOHN 10:10

Letting Go of Resentment

Lord, You know my feelings of resentment against certain people. Forgive me for feeling this way. I won't waste any more time or energy on this. I am only hurting myself by holding on to resentment. Help me to let go of the hurt and anger I feel. I don't want to hold grudges. I don't want this to have power over me any longer. I release them to You. You forgave me, and I choose to forgive them. I have no more desire for revenge. Help me to love them with the love You have shared with me.

Forgive Me for Faking It

Jesus, I've been talking Christianese. I've learned all the right things to say in front of people. They think I'm so spiritual, but I'm lost in the rules of religion. Forgive me for faking it. I desire to have a real relationship with You. Consume me with Your presence. I don't care what others think; my relationship is about You and only You!

> *He will again have compassion on us;*
> *He will tread our iniquities under foot. Yes, You will*
> *cast all their sins into the depths of the sea.*
> MICAH 7:19 NASB

When I've Judged Others

Jesus, please forgive me for judging others. I hate it when others judge me, but it's so easy to condemn, categorize, and criticize the choices others make. Forgive me for being closed-minded, opinionated, self-righteous, and unloving toward the very people You gave Your life for. They are valuable and precious to You. Teach me to see them that way, too. Help me to allow others to express their thoughts and opinions without feeling that my own beliefs are under attack. It is not my place to judge anyone. If possible, let me bring them Your truth in love.

When I've Compromised

Lord, thank You for showing me that the greatest danger to my faith can be when I'm tempted to compromise. Truth isn't negotiable, and I want to be on the side of truth. I don't want to compromise the character, nature, or values that come with my life in Christ. When I do, my old nature leads me instead of Your spirit. Forgive me and help me to stay the course. Guide me in Your truth so I can stand strong, unwilling to compromise.

*So now there is no condemnation for
those who belong to Christ Jesus.*
ROMANS 8:1 NLT

*Courage to Ask
Others for Forgiveness*

God, it is hard to go to others and ask them to forgive me. I can think of all kinds of excuses why I don't have to apologize. The truth is, it's so humbling and embarrassing. Help me to swallow my pride. Give me courage to go to them and be authentic and genuine about my feelings. Help me to face their disappointment, anger, and hurt. Give me words that will help heal our hearts and put things right again, if possible. Teach me to be accountable to others with my words and actions.

A Clean Heart

When people look at my life, I want them to see a heart full of truth. Help me to let go of the hurts hidden deep within my heart. Help me to remove the ugly, hurtful traces of who I used to be instead of who You have helped me become. I want a changed heart. I want to be filled with Your goodness, mercy, and love. I want to become a mirror, reflecting Your image to those around me.

Create in me a clean heart, O God,
and renew a steadfast spirit within me.
PSALM 51:10 NKJV

Forgiveness for the Unforgivable Sin

Father, I feel my sin should be unforgivable. I thought it was the answer to my problems, but since then it's been torturing my mind. The Bible says sin is sin—no matter how small or how big. And I know when I ask for forgiveness, You throw my sin into a sea of forgetfulness and never remember it again. I give You this sin today and I let it go. I refuse to let my past torture me anymore. Thank You for forgiving me and surrounding me with Your love.

When I Feel Betrayed

Jesus, I know You experienced betrayal when Judas kissed You in the garden. What I am experiencing can't compare, but it brings me comfort knowing that You understand. I am hurt and feel so deceived. How can I open myself up and learn to trust someone again? Help me to heal quickly and forgive without compromising myself.

It is no longer I who live, but Christ lives in me. So I live
in this earthly body by trusting in the Son of God,
who loved me and gave himself for me.
GALATIANS 2:20 NLT

When I've Blamed God

God, I've experienced a deep hurt and I didn't know who to blame, so I blamed You. I guess I felt You should have protected me or prevented it from happening. I was just so grieved that I couldn't see the truth. Now I know it wasn't Your fault. Help me to understand what happened. Forgive me for running away from You instead of to You. Thank You for welcoming me into Your open arms even when I was pushing You away. I'm so glad You never gave up on me.

The Benefits of Forgiveness

Heavenly Father, thank You for forgiving me and removing the shame of my sin from me. With all I've done, I am thankful You choose not to hold anything against me. Through Your forgiveness I can enjoy the freedom of Your blessings. And I can forgive myself because You have forgiven me.

Then I heard a loud voice in heaven saying: "The salvation and the power and the kingdom of our God and the authority of his Christ have now come. The accuser of our brothers and sisters, who accused them day and night before our God, has been thrown down."
REVELATION 12:10 NCV

The Ultimate Gift

Lord, thank You for the greatest gift—forgiveness. I am honored to be a recipient of Your mercy. It's a gift I want to share with others. Help me to learn to forgive others easily. You are my example. When I'm tempted to react to the things that hurt and offend me, remind me of Your willingness to forgive me. Teach me to see things from others' perspective. Give me a heart of compassion so I can freely give others the ultimate gift that You have shared with me.

Second Chances

God, You are the God of second chances. Today as I confess my guilt and admit my sins, You are faithful to give me a fresh start. Your mercies are new every morning. Thank You for changing my life by the power of Your heavenly pardon.

> *Everything that we have — right thinking and*
> *right living, a clean slate and a fresh start —*
> *comes from God by way of Jesus Christ.*
> 1 CORINTHIANS 1:30 MSG

My Habits

The Power of a Healthy Lifestyle

Everyone has habits—good and bad. Habits are behaviors you do without thinking about them. They are like simple math: They either add to your life or subtract from it. Do you know someone who pushes everything to the last minute? Procrastinating subtracts from one's life. It robs one of success at work, in relationships, and in achieving one's goals, no matter how small.

What about people who can't hold on to money? No matter how much money they make, it seems to burn a hole in their pockets, and they never have enough. It goes out as fast as it comes in. That habit of spending subtracts from living a healthy financial life.

Then there are those who are committed to adding to their life. Consider the person who demonstrates healthy discipline by eating right and exercising. We know people who pray and feed their spirits regularly. They are growing in their walk with the Lord and they exhibit spiritual strength.

The power of living a healthy life is determined by the positive and negative habits you establish. To achieve your goals, you need to eliminate habits that would take away from your success and to surround yourself with the support that encourages you to add to your life.

The best way to break a bad habit is to replace it with

a good one. Let's say before you became a Christ follower you partied every Saturday night. It's hard to sit at home on Saturdays and think about how much fun your old friends are having. Instead, make a commitment to do something else each Saturday night—join a small group from your church for game night or go to a Saturday night worship service.

Breaking a bad habit is simply choosing something different. Stop doing what you've always done and do something that adds to your life. Become more aware of what you are doing and exercise control over your thoughts, feelings, and actions.

What habits are taking away from various areas of your life? Do you need to be more diligent with your time? Do you need to be a better friend? Take time right now and commit to establishing a new habit.

Ask God to help you develop an action plan that will help you replace the bad habit with a positive one. You don't have to do it alone. God will walk with you through it. Draw on His strength and consider asking someone you trust to help you be accountable. Focus on one habit at a time and work your way to a healthy lifestyle in Christ.

Addressing Bad Habits

Father, I don't want to talk to You about this habit I have, but I know I need to. It makes me want to hide from You. It keeps me from attaining my full potential, and I want to stop. I know I can stop with Your help. Help me to see the real reason for my habit and show me how to heal the pain that drives me to keep doing it. Give me the courage to keep trying if I mess up. Help me to stay strong and just say "no" to guilt.

Forming a Habit of Prayer

I am so thankful that I can talk to You, Lord. Time spent with You in prayer feeds my spirit and fills me with Your power and strength. I am always tempted to come to You with my list of things I want, when I should just sit and listen to what You have to say. Help me to be more diligent with my prayer time.

He [Cornelius] was a thoroughly good man. He had led everyone in his house to live worshipfully before God, was always helping people in need, and had the habit of prayer.
ACTS 10:3 MSG

Making Forgiveness a Habit

God, You always forgive me, but sometimes it's hard to forgive myself. I feel so ashamed when I continue to do things that I've committed to You and myself not to do. The Bible says that once I ask You for forgiveness, You don't remember my sin—but I do. It comes to mind day after day and brings guilt and shame with it. Cleanse my heart and mind of this guilt, Lord. Help me to forgive myself. Help me love myself in spite of my faults—the way You love me.

Add to Your Faith

Father, You have given me great and precious promises. With these promises I can live separate from the world, removed from its evil desires. Because You have given me these blessings, I am determined to add to my faith goodness, knowledge, and self-control today. Help me to grow in patience and in service for You. Help me to show kindness and love to others. As I nurture these things in my life, help me to know You more.

> *Add these things to your lives: to your faith,*
> *add goodness; and to your goodness, add knowledge.*
> 2 PETER 1:5 NCV

Maintaining a Healthy Weight

Lord, I hate to diet. Instead I want to make a lifestyle change. Give me hope to make a lasting change. I can do nothing on my own—I can only be successful when I rely on Your strength. Show me the right choices that will enable me to change. Teach me how to feed my body what it needs instead of what I want. Free me from emotional eating. Give me a new desire to exercise and live a healthy life. Please send people into my life who will encourage me in this commitment.

Self-Speak

God, You know that sometimes I am not nice to myself. I say things that are negative about myself, the way I look and feel. I beat myself up over the choices I make. Teach me to talk to myself as You would. Show me what Your Word says about me. Help me to grow in self-confidence. Show me how to encourage myself in You, like David did. Teach me to talk to myself from Your perspective of who I am.

Words kill, words give life;
they're either poison or fruit—you choose.
PROVERBS 18:21 MSG

Stopping Procrastination

Jesus, I've been so good at putting things off until the last minute. Forgive me! Help me to do the things I should. I want to be ahead instead of behind. Help me to order my day right and to make it a habit to tackle the most obnoxious task first and get it done. When I have the thought, *I'll do it later*, help me to use that thought as a cue that I'm procrastinating. Then give me strength to act fast and do my task right then.

A Habit of Laughter

Father, I haven't had a good belly laugh in a long time. I don't mean to take life too seriously. Bring times of refreshing into my life. Remind me to look for opportunities to experience the joy of laughter. Point them out to me and then help me to let go and have a good time. Laughter seems to release stress and adjust my attitude. Inject me with funny thoughts when I need to relax and have a good laugh.

Windows of My Soul

Lord, one image can affect my thoughts for days. Give me wisdom to protect my heart and mind from the things I should not see. Help me to avoid things that would hurt my heart.

"Let's not pretend this is easier than it really is. If you want to live a morally pure life, here's what you have to do: You have to blind your right eye the moment you catch it in a lustful leer. You have to choose to live one-eyed or else be dumped on a moral trash pile."
MATTHEW 5:29 MSG

Devoted to Truth

Lord, when I am devoted to Your truth, it becomes clear what things do and don't belong in my life. I don't want to believe the lie that truth is relative. Show me truth in black and white. Help me to break the habits that keep me from living a life pleasing to You. As I am tempted to repeat an old habit, remind me that You are there with me, ready to help me let go. Help me to live according to Your truth.

Life in Your Word

God, Your Word breathes life into me. Help me to be committed to Your Word, to study it, and place it in my heart. Bring Your words back to me as I go through my day. Instruct me, encourage me, and fill me with Your words.

My son, pay attention to what I say; listen closely to my words. Do not let them out of your sight, keep them within your heart; for they are life to those who find them and health to a man's whole body.
PROVERBS 4:20–22

Relationship Habits

Father, I have a bad habit of needing others to pay attention to me. I want them to notice and speak to me. My confidence should come from knowing You and believing I will become who You created me to be. I don't need the approval of others, especially those I don't know. Speak to me when I do this. Help me to stop. Show me how to turn my focus from myself to them. I can't show Your love to others if I'm seeking something from them. Help me to establish good relationship habits.

A Habit of Selflessness

Lord, I've been self-centered. There are times when I felt like the world revolved around me. Forgive me for such selfishness. I won't die if everything doesn't go my way. Help me not to react so emotionally when something doesn't turn out as I expected. Give me compassion for others and a sense of selflessness to serve them.

Since Jesus went through everything you're going through and more, learn to think like him. Think of your sufferings as a weaning from that old sinful habit of always expecting to get your own way.
1 PETER 4:1 MSG

The Power to Change

Help me, Lord, to focus on the positive qualities that I have and the Word of God that describes me in the light of Your love. I am an overcomer in Christ Jesus. I am a new creature in Christ, with new thoughts, intents, and purposes. My mind is made new as I spend time with You. Remind me of just how much You love me. I rely on Your strength to help me to make the changes I need to make today.

My Responsibilities

The Power of Commitment

Have you ever been disappointed when someone didn't follow through on a commitment they made to you? When someone trustworthy makes a promise to you, you normally develop an expectation that the promise will be fulfilled. Do you keep every promise you make? Are you responsible for your actions and words?

You can count on God to keep His promises and commitments. Our very world—the earth we walk, the air we breathe, and the water that sustains us—was created by His Word. God's Word holds everything together, and if the devil could get God to break His Word, just one time, all creation would cease to exist.

You are created in God's image, and your word has power. The more you protect your word and do what you say you will do, the more power your word has in your life and in the lives of those who trust you. Do you disappoint others with promises you can't keep? Excuses are just that—excuses. No matter how valid those excuses are, others will remember whether or not you followed through on your commitment.

You need people you can count on to keep their commitments, and your family and friends need to be able to count on you when you take on responsibility. They need to know you're going to deliver. And God needs to know that He can count on you, too.

Responsible people know the importance of counting the cost before they make a commitment that would make them responsible for the outcome. They count the cost.

The Book of Esther is a beautiful story of a young woman who counted the cost. She knew she could die if she approached the king without him first summoning her, but still she took action at the risk of her own life to save her people.

Jesus told us to count the cost before we build (Luke 14:28). Every day you build your life. You add to or take away from who you are becoming. Any responsibility you take on should be considered carefully before you commit to it. Ask yourself what it's going to cost if you do it, and what it's going to cost if you don't. There's always a cost—spiritually, emotionally, relationally, financially, and even physically.

Ask God to help you count the cost and, with His direction, commit to the things that will add to your life here on earth today and for all eternity.

Accepting Responsibility for My Actions

It would be easier to deny my mistakes to myself and to others, but I want to be a person of integrity and honor. Truth is important to You—and to me. Lord, give me the courage to take responsibility for my actions. I know that with each action there are consequences, both positive and negative. Help me to think before I act and to listen to Your instruction and direction for decisions I make, no matter how big or small.

> *"Great gifts mean great responsibilities;*
> *greater gifts, greater responsibilities!"*
> LUKE 12:48 MSG

Accepting Responsibility for My Words

My words are powerful—they can add to or take away from someone's life. I want to be a positive influence in the lives of those around me. I want to encourage them with Your goodness and love. I want to be truthful, and sometimes it's hard to say certain things, but I'm asking You to help me speak the truth in love. For those I have hurt with my words, help me to take responsibility, apologize, and set things right with them. Lord, put a guard over my mouth so I speak Your words in love.

Keeping Promises to Myself

Lord, You created me for a specific purpose. I make promises to myself and think it's okay not to keep them. Help me to remember that I'm responsible to You for how my life turns out. Help me to keep the commitments I've set and give me the courage to accomplish them. Remind me that it's okay to do good things for myself that help me to become the person You created me to be.

> *Each of you must take responsibility for doing*
> *the creative best you can with your own life.*
> GALATIANS 6:5 MSG

Making Realistic Commitments

Father, I want to live a balanced life. I am tired of people pulling at me. Show me how to choose what is important and necessary. Give me strength to say "no" when something doesn't belong on my list. I can't do everything that is asked of me. Help me to see what's important and when it's important. I want to remain stable in my spiritual, physical, emotional, relational, and financial needs. Teach me how to negotiate my time and energy—leaving plenty of time for rest and fun while doing what is necessary in all the other areas of my life.

When I'm Tempted to Take Shortcuts

God, people around me take moral shortcuts, but I know that isn't right for me. You have given me values of honor, integrity, and truth. Help me not to compromise. Although others may act without integrity as they climb the corporate ladder, it's not worth the price of my relationship with You to follow their example. You bless me because I choose what is right and just. Thank You for reminding me of the way I need to go.

For we cannot oppose the truth,
but must always stand for the truth.
2 CORINTHIANS 13:8 NLT

When I'm Afraid to Commit

I don't know what to do. I have a huge decision in front of me but it means a high level of commitment. There's so much pressure to make a decision while I don't have all the facts. I'm conflicted and confused, but Your Word says that confusion is not of You. Help me to press through all the confusing clutter of this situation. Shine Your light on it and show me what You want me to do. Then if it's right, I'll do whatever it takes to be accountable, to see this thing through.

When I Break a Promise

I did it again—I failed; I broke a promise. I feel guilty and ashamed. I thought I could pull it off but I've hurt someone and disappointed myself and You. Forgive me for not counting the cost and thinking I could manage this alone. Give me the courage to apologize and correct my mistake, whatever it takes. Please comfort the people I hurt and help them to forgive me and maybe let me try again.

Good people will be guided by honesty;
dishonesty will destroy those who are not trustworthy.
PROVERBS 11:3 NCV

Keeping Commitments to Friends

I don't mean to take advantage of others, but I've done it. Forgive me for it. Jesus, open my eyes to see that I hurt my friends when I'm late, cancel, or just don't show up. Let me see this before it's too late to keep my commitments. Teach me how to schedule for interruptions and still keep the appointments that are most important on the schedule.

You yourself must be an example to them by doing good works of every kind. Let everything you do reflect the integrity and seriousness of your teaching. Teach the truth so that your teaching can't be criticized. Then those who oppose us will be ashamed and have nothing bad to say about us.
TITUS 2:7–8 NLT

Commitment to Prayer

I get so busy with so many things that I often lose track of time and forget about You. Forgive me. I'm so sorry. I know You wait patiently for me to spend time with You. I'm asking You to remind me, prompt me, call to me. I promise to be more diligent with my time with You. You know everything there is to know about me. You hold all the answers for my life in the palm of Your hand. Help me to come to You, sit at Your feet, and listen carefully to the answers You have for my life questions.

Keeping Commitments at Work

Jesus, some people on my team are difficult to work with. Their ideas are different and their values are questionable, yet we have to succeed together. I have commitments to them that are hard to keep. Help me to represent You on the team. Show me how to fulfill my commitments by Your standards. Help me to serve my team members as You would serve them. Remind me that we succeed or fail only as a team.

Enlisting the Help of Others

Lord, why is it so hard sometimes to ask for help? I don't want people to think I'm weak or that the task is too hard. Change my perception of needing help. Give me a new understanding: Asking for help doesn't mean I am weak, but that I value relationship with others. It says that I have confidence in their ability to assist me. Even when I need help from strangers, give me the courage to ask and to handle the rejection if they say "no." Grant me approval by those I ask for help.

No More Excuses

When I refuse to accept personal responsibility, I create my own problems. Lord, forgive me when I blame others for my situation instead of taking necessary steps to change my circumstances. Help me to accept my mistakes, look at them realistically, and learn from them. Help me find the courage in You to embrace my personal responsibility and see it as an opportunity to grow. Give me strength to make responsible choices. Guide me with Your wisdom in all I do and help me see the truth of my actions clearly.

Counting the Cost

Everything I do or don't do costs me something—time, effort, emotional energy. When I choose, Lord, help me find balance. Will this added responsibility add to my life, add value to my relationships, or help me to achieve a higher standard of living at the cost of my health? Give me a reality check with each commitment I consider making.

> *"For even if the mountains walk away and the hills*
> *fall to pieces, my love won't walk away from you,*
> *my covenant commitment of peace won't fall apart."*
> *The God who has compassion on you says so.*
> ISAIAH 54:10 MSG

God's Commitment to Me

Lord, You are great! I want the whole world to know what You have done for me. You have changed my life and set me free. I was lost and alone, and You found me. Everything I need is in You. You created me and crowned me with Your glory. You take responsibility for me, whether I succeed or fail. From the beginning of time, every promise You have made, You have kept. Generation after generation depends on You, just as I do.

> *Remember his covenant forever—*
> *the commitment he made to a thousand generations.*
> 1 CHRONICLES 16:15 NLT

My Time

The Power of Priorities

No doubt going to school has taken up a lot of your time and has been a priority. With graduation behind you, it's important to take a serious look at how you should spend your time now. What are your priorities over the next few days, weeks, or years?

It's important to be purposeful with your time. Every person on the planet has the same amount of time each day. You have to learn to manage yourself, because time refuses to be managed. *Time* management is really *self*-management—learning to use the inflexible twenty-four hours of the day in ways that best help you accomplish your goals.

No one can change time, so you must continually remain aware of it. There are tools available to help you be more conscious of your time: clocks, watches, calendars, personal organizers, seminars, and computer programs. And still, we often find it difficult to make time to do everything we have to do.

Think of time as a currency—where do you spend it? Who or what will you give your time to today? Is that time wisely invested? You can probably think of many occasions when you let time get away from you. We've all looked up from a project or activity and realized we'd spent much more time on what we were doing than we intended.

Jesus said, "Wherever your treasure is, there the desires of your heart will also be" (Matthew 6:21 NLT). So how and where you choose to spend your time says a lot about what is most important to you.

The key to successful self-management is in setting priorities. Think back over the past few days. How did you spend your time, effort, and energy? Did you have a goal you were pushing to reach? Likely your focus was on getting through graduation.

We need to allocate our time based on what we believe to be most important. Are our friends and family important? Then we schedule time for them. We *invest* our time in them.

As we read the Bible, it becomes clear that we are God's greatest priority. He has spent much of His time focused on bringing us back into relationship with Him.

Your relationship with God is the foundation of your success in everything else you do. All you will ever need is found in your relationship with Him. As you grow in Him, you become strong, healthy, and full of His love, and then you are able to overflow into the lives of others.

Through prayer and commitment to your relationship with God, He can help you make every minute count. He can help you focus on the things that are most important to you and to Him.

The First Priority

Father, You are my everything! Without You, I wouldn't even be here. Forgive me for allowing so many other things to squeeze between me and You. Help me to become more diligent in my time with You. It fills me with the strength I need to make it day after day. I love You so much! I never want to take our relationship for granted.

> " 'Love the Lord your God with all your heart
> and with all your soul and with all your mind.'
> This is the first and greatest commandment."
> MATTHEW 22:37–38

Making Prayer a Priority

God, I am reaching out to You from the deepest places in my heart. I love You and want to make prayer a favorite part of my day. Help me to be consistent in spending time with You. Teach me to recognize and reject the distractions and the unending list of things that keep me too busy for You. My relationship with You is my highest priority and strongest commitment. Remind me of that and give me the determination to spend time in prayer no matter what situations arise. Let nothing keep me from You!

Living in the Now

I can't change the past, but I think about it a lot. It's a waste of time, and I hate for my mind to go there. I don't want to recount my past mistakes—I've been forgiven. Lord, help me to focus on today. Help me to keep my attention on the priorities You have given me. Help me to live in the present. Show me what I can do today to make an eternal difference.

> *"And the second [greatest commandment] is like it:*
> *'Love your neighbor as yourself.'"*
> MATTHEW 22:39

Every Minute Counts

What I do today affects my tomorrow. Lord, help me to be conscious of time-wasters. I don't want to be idle and lazy. Show me Your plan and the things I need to put my hands to, but at the same time help me to balance my life so I take good care of my body and mind with the right amount of rest. As I walk with You, I know I am pursuing the things You want me to do. I ask You to help me be in the right place at the right time every time.

When Others Fail Me

When others fail me, it makes me feel unimportant to them. It hurts my feelings and I want to be angry. Remind me of the times when circumstances were out of my control and I missed a commitment and failed someone. Fill me with compassion and understanding for their situation. Help me to get over it and show them Your love.

Make allowance for each other's faults, and forgive anyone who offends you. Remember, the Lord forgave you, so you must forgive others.
COLOSSIANS 3:13 NLT

When I Make Excuses

God, I know You aren't about excuses, but I make them when I don't want to do something I need to do. Forgive me for not being diligent. Give me strength to tackle the difficult tasks first, even those things I find boring. Help me to do the things I don't want to do as if I were doing them for You. That would give the job more purpose, at least for me. And remind me never to leave a job unfinished that I've committed to do. I want to leave a good impression on others, especially when I'm representing You.

When I'm Overcommitted

God, I did it again—I'm overcommitted, stressed, and overwhelmed. Someone I made a promise to is going to be disappointed in me. Why can't I just say "no" to start with? Help me to manage better and be realistic about what I can accomplish in one day. Give me wisdom when others ask me to help them. It's better to say "no" and help later, if I can, than to make a promise and then let someone down who was counting on me. When I make promises, help me to have the integrity to keep them.

Sacrifices

I only have so much time every day. Lord, help me to spend my time wisely, on the things that matter most. Day-to-day things are continually in my face, screaming for my attention, but there are also things that are eternal, like people. Help me realize my time spent for eternal things, like spending time with others, is not a sacrifice, but a reward.

> *You were taught to be made new in your hearts,*
> *to become a new person. That new person is made to*
> *be like God—made to be truly good and holy.*
> EPHESIANS 4:23–24 NCV

When I'm Distracted

Lord, my mind is wandering again. Help me to stay focused on what I have in front of me. I have the mind of Christ and I am determined to stay steady until I've finished the task. I will not look to the right or the left. I refuse to be distracted. I push my worries to the side. I will accomplish what I've set my heart to do. I will not quit. I have a mission and I will achieve it.

Getting the Most out of My Day

Father, when I was a child a day seemed so long that sometimes I got bored. Now, I find there are not enough hours to complete what I need to do each day. I need Your wisdom about how to budget my time. Show me how I can use it more efficiently.

But most of all, my brothers and sisters, never take an oath, by heaven or earth or anything else. Just say a simple yes or no, so that you will not sin and be condemned.
JAMES 5:12 NLT

Enjoying Time Alone

God, sometimes I feel guilty when I make time to be alone. My relationships are important to me, but time alone is important, too. Jesus took time to get away and be alone. Teach me to follow His example. Remind me to spend that time reflecting on the many good things You have done in my life. Remembering those times helps me to grow stronger in my faith. Time alone is a great opportunity to study Your Word and let You minister to me. Help me to enjoy my alone time with You.

Tools for Time

Lord, help me to find tools to make me more effective in the use of my time. Bring the right people across my path to educate me about how to use the tools that best fit my personality and gifts.

Instruct them to do good, to be rich in good works, to be generous and ready to share, storing up for themselves the treasure of a good foundation for the future, so they may take hold of that which is life indeed.
1 TIMOTHY 6:18–19 NASB

Knowing What's Important

Now that I've graduated, I'm facing new demands on my time and energy. Father, help me to know what is most important. I know that growing in my relationship with You is first, so I need Your help in staying true to that commitment. Second, I need Your help in valuing the relationships You bring into my life and caring for them with the power of Your love. Please tap me on the shoulder and remind me when I'm becoming too busy. I don't want to miss the most important priorities in life.

The Right Time

Father, I have lots of ideas. There's so much I want to do, but I just don't know when to do it. Your timing is everything. You have ordered my steps, and You know the way that I should go. I ask the Holy Spirit to lead and guide me. Give me assurance and peace to know when it's time to step forward. Thank You for making everything happen in Your time, not mine.

People can make all kinds of plans,
but only the Lord's plan will happen.
PROVERBS 19:21 NCV

The Power of Expectation

Steve Jobs, CEO for Apple, Inc., said, "The people who are crazy enough to think they can change the world are the ones who do." If you think about it, his words are true. Consider all the people who attempted something they were told they never could do, but succeeded. Now, that success may have come only after many failures at trying to achieve that dream.

The most important thing to realize is whether or not the dream is God-given. When our dreams line up with God's will for our lives, then we can trust Him to meet our expectations. God's ways are higher than our ways and sometimes we have to let his plan play out without interfering. It helps not to hold so tightly to what you've imagined it to be, but instead remain open to the way God wants to do it. Sometimes the way we want to go isn't the same road God wants us to take. Ephesians 3:20 NKJV says God "is able to do exceedingly abundantly above all that we ask or think." What if our asking and thinking fall short of what we are able to do or become? The power to achieve your goals and dreams isn't in the dream itself but in the expectation that God is faithful to make it happen!

Another reason we miss the goal that God has for our lives is because we quit. "Let us not become weary in doing good, for at the proper time we will reap a harvest if we do not give up" (Galatians 6:9). There will always be opposition to our faith, challenging us and questioning if we *truly* believe. We have to hold fast to the promises of God and trust Him to carry us through.

It takes prayer and commitment to see God's plan for your live revealed. God lives beyond your expectations—the more you trust Him for His very best, the higher you can go. What would happen in your life today if you *really* let go and let God take you where He desires you to go? When you continue to press forward with the expectation that He'll see you through, His dreams for your life can become reality.

The Power to Believe

Father, I have many dreams but I've also experienced disappointment. I want to believe I can achieve my dreams. When I'm discouraged, help me to remember that all things are possible when I believe. I know Your expectations for my life are greater than I can imagine. Bring me back to Your promises when I'm tempted to think I can't achieve, because Your Word says I can do all things through Christ who gives me strength. I draw on that strength now for courage to push forward.

Christ's Return

Lord, forgive me. I say I'm a Christian and that I believe in You, but my focus is so much on today that I don't live like I expect You to return at any moment. You should be my focus, and Your return is what I should look forward to. Remind me of the eternal. Help me to remember that this world is not my home and that my journey is just beginning with You.

> *"You also must be ready all the time, for the*
> *Son of Man will come when least expected."*
> LUKE 12:40 NLT

High Expectations

My high expectations can leave me disappointed. Sometimes I'm disappointed because I imagine how You're going to work everything out for me, yet the outcome doesn't look like I thought it would. It freaks me out at first because I'm afraid all I've hoped for won't happen. But then You outdo Yourself and it's better than I could ever imagine. Forgive me for my doubt. Remind me of Your faithfulness. Help me to trust You from the time I pray to the time I receive Your answer.

Unmet Expectations

Lord, my expectations were high, and I'm so disappointed in what looks to be the outcome of this situation. Help me to remember that You are in control. I've given this situation to You. Help me to let go of it once again. You are faithful and just and You always deliver what You promise. It doesn't look like what I expected, but I'm learning that Your way is always better in the end.

Let us hold tightly without wavering to the hope we affirm,
for God can be trusted to keep his promise.
HEBREWS 10:23 NLT

To Dream Again

Lord, You know all the big dreams I once had for the future. I don't want to admit it, but I've given up on my dreams. They seemed so impossible and my desire to see them through slowly faded away. I want to dream again. I want to experience the future You planned for me. Give me a red-hot fire for my dream that won't go out. Show me those people who will support my endeavors and please shield me from those who won't. Give me Your supernatural grace, peace, and endurance to achieve my dream.

Pursuing My Dream

You gave me a gift, and I want to use it to begin the work You have for me to do. Your only Son, Jesus, knew His mission while on the earth, and He completed it. Father, give me the drive, power, and determination to accomplish my mission. I am committed and ready to pursue my dream. Thank You for the courage to move forward. I am stepping out in faith today.

I press toward the goal for the prize
of the upward call of God in Christ Jesus.
PHILIPPIANS 3:14 NKJV

Getting Back on Track

Lord, I fully believe I was born with God-given purpose, but I feel like my life is going nowhere. There's got to be more! I feel displaced, like I stepped off Your road map for my life. There's a fire burning within me to get back on track. Help me to remove the distractions and focus on You. I want to hear Your voice and go where You are leading me. I'm begging You, intervene in my life today. I'm willing and committed to doing what You tell me to do. Help me find my place.

When I'm Tired

God, I've been pushing myself hard to graduate. I need some downtime. I don't want to grow weary and quit, but I need some breathing room. Help me to take time to rest and relax. It seems I've faced so many obstacles in pursuit of this dream. I know I can do it. Refresh me today with Your presence. Fill me with Your peace and restore me in Your love. As soon as I gain the strength to press on, I'll take another breath and dive in, pressing hard to reach my goals again.

To See It Through

I've imagined my life in different ways, but it isn't turning out as I thought it would. I've found rough waters at every turn. You never said it would be easy, but You have promised to do exceedingly more than I can imagine. Help me to see this dream through to reality. Show me what it looks like from Your perspective. Help me not to fall short, but to rise to the level You desire me to reach.

The way of the good person is like the light of dawn,
growing brighter and brighter until full daylight.
PROVERBS 4:18 NCV

Sharing My Dream with Others

Father, sometimes I get disappointed when I share my dream with others. People can be negative, and hearing their lack of enthusiasm over and over discourages me. I need people who will be excited about my plans. Give me wisdom in whom I share my dream with. Teach me how to overcome negativity. Please show me Your words of wisdom that will build me up in faith. Bring supporters who will cheer me on as I race for the prize of accomplishment. And more than anything, remind me that my confidence is in You.

When I Drag My Feet

Why am I procrastinating in moving forward? Is that me or You? Speak to my heart, Lord. What is set before me seems hard. And maybe I'm a little afraid, but You are with me. I don't want to miss anything You have prepared for me, but I'm willing to wait for Your leading. I need to know Your timing on this. Give me wisdom and tell me when to jump in.

Lazy people want much but get little,
but those who work hard will prosper.
PROVERBS 13:4 NLT

Commitment to God's Dream

Lord, I'm ready to make a commitment to work with You to fulfill the plan You have for my life. All that You have asked of me, I will do. Thank You that I don't have to do anything alone. You are always here with me. You make the resources I need available to me to get the job done. I'm trusting You to give me strength when I jump the hurdles before me. No matter what I need, You have the answer. I commit my work to You, Lord. I trust You to establish it and set me firm on a foundation of faith.

Removing the Limits

Father, You have promised to hear me when I pray and to honor me as I serve You. We're doing this together. I am removing the limits that have constrained me in the past. It doesn't matter what other people think; my heart is tuned to Your voice. I hear Your words, and I determine never to follow a discouraging voice. Nothing is impossible with You.

Listen to my voice in the morning, LORD. Each morning
I bring my requests to you and wait expectantly.
PSALM 5:3 NLT

Patience for the Dream

God, I want to see results quickly, but I understand that's not realistic. I need to give You time to work behind the scenes. It would be so much easier to wait if I knew the details from Your perspective, but that's not faith. Forgive me when I want to take control, or when I try to make things happen on my own time line. Help me to stand strong, believing that the final outcome is exactly what You want it to be. I trust You, knowing You will get us to our dream.

My Future

The Power of Pursuing God's Plan

Now that you're a graduate, do family and friends look at you as if you should have a plan for the rest of your life? It can be overwhelming when people ask you to present them with the complete blueprint for your future. The truth is, all of us feel lost at times. A comedian once said, "The reason why adults ask children what they want to be when they grow up is because they're looking for suggestions!" Even with the title of recent graduate, it's okay to admit you don't have all the answers.

God created you to succeed. We can get so busy pursuing our future that we can forget that His ways are higher than our ways. Jeremiah 29:11 says "'For I know the plans I have for you,' declares the LORD, 'plans to prosper you and not to harm you, plans to give you hope and a future.'" We're all guilty of coming up with our own plans, putting them into action, and then hoping and praying that God will bless them.

We all have great plans for our futures. And since God doesn't give us a personal course description laid out word for word for the rest of our lives, we can be tempted to go our own way. *My way or God's way?* It makes sense that the Creator of the universe would have the ultimate plan for our lives; yet, we often struggle for control. Frankly, it's a scary feeling to relinquish total control of our lives to someone we can't see or touch. Faith requires that we live one day at a time following His lead.

At first glance you might think David had it made as a young man. After all, he knew his future—God said he would be the next king of Israel. Although his own family never considered him a candidate, God promised him the throne.

David's story begins in 1 Samuel 16 when he is called in from tending his father's sheep and anointed as the next king of Israel. His future probably didn't play out like he imagined—he didn't go from the sheep pasture immediately to the throne. He had to hold tightly to the promise God had given him. It took many years, and David experienced failures alongside great victories before he ever wore his crown.

No doubt David asked God the same questions you've asked: *When? Why? How? Are You still there? Is this still Your will for my life?* The prayers and cries of David's heart are recorded in many of the psalms as he pursued God's plan for his future.

Maybe, like David, you know what you want to do with your life. Perhaps you've had a passion for something since you were a child, but now as a graduate you're finding that God's plan looks different from yours.

God is always faithful to lead and guide you. God has set your course, and it's okay if you don't know every single detail of His plan. Take time to pray, and follow His directions one day at a time.

Waiting on the Future

Just as You promised David that he would be king, You have made promises to me for my life. I know everything You promised will happen, and I'm excited about the future. It's hard to wait on the future I know You have planned for me. Help me to find patience to be content doing what I should be doing now while on my way to achieving the purpose You have for my life.

Know also that wisdom is sweet to your soul; if you find it,
there is a future hope for you, and your hope will not be cut off.
PROVERBS 24:14

Graduation Prayer

God, as I move forward, help me to pursue the future You have for me. I'll find my place and achieve the assignments You give me. All I ask is that You be with me every step of the way, and I know You will. Help me stay on course and use every gift You have given me for Your divine plan. Help me to choose Your ways over my own feelings and opinions. Remind me to run to Your Word and find the answers I need. And never, never let me quit!

Revealing of God's Plan

Father, You have placed Your purposes deep within my heart. When I look inside myself now, help me see only what You have planned for me. Give me courage to step out with confidence, knowing that You perfect everything that concerns me.

"Eye has not seen, nor ear heard, nor have entered into the heart of man the things which God has prepared for those who love Him." But God has revealed them to us through His Spirit. For the Spirit searches all things, yes, the deep things of God.
1 CORINTHIANS 2:9–10 NKJV

Finding God's Plan for Marriage

Lord, I want Your answers for my life. Show me Your purpose and plan for marriage. Prepare me for my future spouse by showing me the issues in my life that I need to correct now so I am ready to love and be loved without emotional baggage or restraints. Heal me from damaged emotions and past hurts so I don't take those things into my marriage. Bring the person into my life that You chose for me and make your choice clear to me when Your time is right.

Giving God Control of My Future

Jesus, You knew that God's will was for You to give Your life so that others may experience God. You gave God total control and submitted to His will. Help me to do the same. I was created for a specific purpose. You have a plan for my life, and I want to complete everything You created me to accomplish. Help me to live my life according to Your ultimate plan.

We plan the way we want to live,
but only GOD makes us able to live it.
PROVERBS 16:9 MSG

Prayer of Discernment

That same Spirit who raised Christ from the dead lives in me. Thank You that my heart is sensitive to Your purposes and plans for my life. I clearly distinguish between right and wrong; I see the light and walk in it. I trust You, Lord, with all my heart and refuse to rely on my own understanding in any matter. Help me to choose Your way, the right way, every time. I am determined to know You and discern Your voice when You're speaking to me, just as a child knows the voice of a parent.

God's Plan of Blessing

The Bible tells me that whatever I put my hand to will prosper. I am blessed in the city and in the field, when I come into my house, and when I go out of it. Your blessing on my life provides for my every need. I ask for Your wisdom, Lord. Teach me to make the right choices and decisions for my life. You make me a blessing because I belong to You.

> *"I am the LORD your God, who teaches you to profit,*
> *who leads you in the way you should go."*
> ISAIAH 48:17 NASB

Walking Toward Your Destiny

Sometimes my life feels upside-down, and I need You to come along and flip it right-side up. Point me in the right direction; place me directly on Your path for my life. Please don't let me miss a beat. Help me to be willing always to walk with You toward my destiny. When I become distracted or make a wrong turn, sound the alarm of my heart and I will run to You. Set my feet back on the right course and keep me moving in the right direction.

Moving to a New Location

Change is hard, and moving to a new place is frightening and exciting at the same time. You know what awaits me at my new location. Give me a good start with everyone I meet. Help me to make an easy transition. Lord, prepare friendships in this new location, people who will inspire and encourage me in my faith. Help me to find a church where I can feel at home with others and with You. I trust You with all my heart and know that You have orchestrated each step as I follow You.

Looking Forward

Sometimes I look back at the things that didn't turn out quite right for me. I know I shouldn't focus on wrongs done to me or opportunities missed. You have set a great life before me, and I want to embrace it without the shadow of the past. Help me see the future with joy and expectation. My hope is in *You!*

"When the Spirit of truth comes, he will guide you into all truth. He will not speak on his own but will be tell you what he has heard. He will tell you about the future."
JOHN 16:13 NLT

Future Success

The Bible encourages me to store my treasures in heaven, and I want to do that, but You have also promised me success here on earth. Today I ask You for wisdom in everything I do. Help me to live my life with honor and integrity so I can bring glory to Your name. Teach me Your ways so I continually walk in Your blessings. Thank You for causing others to respect me because I am a reflection of You. I pray others see something in me that sets me apart and points them to You.

Planning Ahead

You know my life gets so busy that I seem to get stuck in the moment. Remind me to lift up my head and look to the future. Help me to have realistic and attainable goals. Show me how to balance my life for today while at the same time planning for tomorrow. Remind me to set my eyes on You so I can see where we're going together, with my future on the horizon.

The ants are not a strong people,
but they prepare their food in the summer.
PROVERBS 30:25 NASB

News of Unsettled Future

Lord, the news reports cause so many of us to worry: economic downturns, threats of terrorism, wars, and natural disasters. You are my rock and my safety. I know as long as I hold tight to You that I have a future. You are my help in times of trouble, and I trust You to keep me steady. Lord, help me to doubt my doubt and to stand strong, knowing that You hold my future in Your hands. I fix my eyes on You and follow Your leading. You perfect everything that concerns me. You hold my future in Your hands.

The Power of Recognizing Seasons

Father, I know there is a season for everything. I was born at the right season and this is my time to live a great life. The Bible tells me there is a time for every purpose under heaven—a time to weep, a time to laugh, a time to mourn, and a time to dance. Help me to recognize the season I am in and help me to flow with it. I don't want to be resistant. Show me how to bend with Your leading.

To everything there is a season,
a time for every purpose under heaven.
ECCLESIASTES 3:1 NKJV

Conclusion

Putting the Power of Prayer to Work

In my anguish I cried to the LORD,
and he answered by setting me free.
PSALM 118:5

The Bible is full of examples of God's provision through the prayers of those who called on His name. Take, for instance, the prophet Elijah, who obeyed God by proclaiming truth to God's people during difficult times. In 1 Kings 17, a godly widow who opened her home to Elijah went to him to lament her son's illness and death.

> She said to Elijah, "What do you have against me, man of God? Did you come to remind me of my sin and kill my son?"
>
> "Give me your son," Elijah replied. He took him from her arms, carried him to the upper room where he was staying, and laid him on his bed. Then he cried out to the LORD, "O LORD my God, have you brought tragedy also upon this widow I am staying with, by causing her son to die?" Then he stretched himself out on the boy three times and cried to the LORD, "O LORD my God, let this boy's life return to him!"
>
> The LORD heard Elijah's cry, and the boy's life returned to him, and he lived. Elijah picked up the child and carried him down from the room into the house. He gave him to his mother and said, "Look, your son is alive!"

Then the woman said to Elijah, "Now I know that you are a man of God and that the word of the LORD from your mouth is the truth" (1 Kings 17:18–24).

As you move from graduation to the next milepost in your life, God wants to share every day with you. When you speak to Him in prayer, He is listening. He has the answers to the questions you face in life. Every person is different, and the questions you will ask on your journey are unique to you and are important to your pursuit of God's best.

Throughout these pages, hopefully you have discovered the open door to relationship with God through prayer and have taken the opportunity to invite Him in.

Were you surprised to find that God wants to share your life with you? When you choose to agree with God's desires and plans in prayer and declaration, you choose to live with the authority and dominion God originally created His people to experience on the earth.

Conversation with God through prayer has the power to transform you and make lasting changes in your life. As you invite the Holy Spirit to make the Word of God real to your heart and mind, you get to know God in a real way. Soon your prayer times will be powerful moments in which you honestly and openly express to God who you are and who God is to you.

Continue to allow times of prayer to guide you in every area of life. Your time spent with your heavenly Father will give you the direction you need every day of your life.